Glencoe

Course 1

The McGraw·Hill Companies

Send all inquiries to:
Glencoe/McGraw-Hill
8787 Orion Place
Columbus, OH 43240-4027

ISBN (student edition): 978-0-07-889198-4
MHID (student edition): 0-07-889198-1
Printed in the United States of America.

2 3 4 5 6 7 8 9 110/043 14 13 12 11 10 09

Program Consultants

Dr. Diane August
Educational Researcher

- Principal investigator, Developing Literacy in Second-Language Learners: Report of the National Literacy Panel on Language-Minority Children and Youth
- Member of the New Standards Literacy Project, Grades 4–5

Dr. Jana Echevarria
California State University, Long Beach

- Author of *Making Content Comprehensible for English Learners: The SIOP Model*
- Principal Researcher, Center for Research on the Educational Achievement and Teaching of English Language Learners

Dr. Donald R. Bear
University of Nevada, Reno

- Author of *Words Their Way* and *Words Their Way with English Learners*
- Director, E.L. Cord Foundation Center for Learning and Literacy

Carol Rothenberg
Project Resource Teacher

Office of Language Acquisition San Diego USD

Co-author, *Teaching English Language Learners: A Differentiated Approach*

Co-author, *Language Learners in the English Classroom*

San Diego, CA

CONTENTS

Helping Others

Talk About It!

What beliefs help guide you in life?

READ
- Buddhism
- Mahatma Gandhi: The Salt March

Prepare To Read

Text Structure: Comparing and Contrasting

Text structure is the order or pattern of ideas in a text. Comparing and contrasting is one way an author can organize text. **Comparing** means telling how things are the same. **Contrasting** means telling how things are different. Look for the following signal words and phrases as you read:

❱ Signal words for comparing—*similar, like,* and *also*

❱ Signal words for contrasting—*but, however,* and *on the other hand*

Practice Read the paragraph. What words tell you that the text structure is comparing and contrasting?

> What activities do you enjoy? Some activities take place indoors. For example, people watch TV and visit museums indoors. But other activities take place outdoors, such as fishing and hiking.

Reading Skill **Determine Main Idea and Supporting Details**

The **main idea** is the most important idea in a paragraph or a text. **Supporting details** are ideas that tell more about the main idea.

To **determine main idea and supporting details**, ask yourself:

❱ What is each sentence or paragraph about?

❱ What idea do most of the sentences support?

As you read, complete the graphic organizer in the *Expressions Practice Book.*

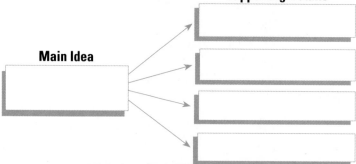

Main Idea

Supporting Details

Vocabulary for Buddhism

Read the words and definitions below.

desires (di zī rz') *n.* When you have **desires** for things, you want them very badly.
Cognate (Spanish) **deseos**

meditate (me' də tāt) *v.* When you **meditate**, you keep your body still and focus your mind.
Cognate (Spanish) **meditar**

fame (fām') *n.* You have **fame** when many people know who you are. Cognate (Spanish) **fama**

suffering (sə' fər ing) *n.* **Suffering** is a situation when one person or many people experience pain or difficulty.
Cognate (Spanish) **sufrimiento**

follow (fä' lō) *v.* When you **follow** someone, you go where they go or do what they do.

wisdom (wiz' dəm) *n.* **Wisdom** is a deep understanding of people and ideas that comes from life experience.

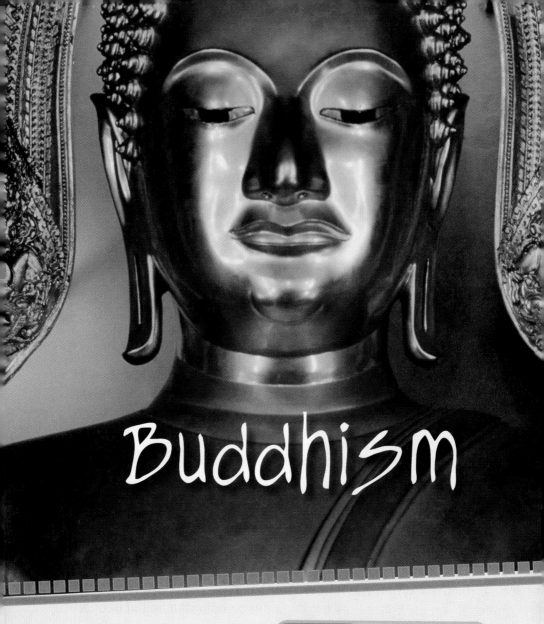

Buddhism

READ To Find Out > Who created Buddhism?

Sometimes you want things that you cannot have. How does that make you feel? Siddhartha Gautama asked these questions around 600 B.C. (before the time of Jesus Christ). The answers he found are now called Buddhism. Many people around the world practice Buddhism to find their own answers.

Who is the Buddha?

Siddhartha Gautama was born in what is now Nepal (nə pôl) about 563 B.C. He had everything he wanted. He was a rich prince. He had a wife and son. One day Siddhartha decided to leave his **palace**. For the first time, he saw poor people. He saw sick people. He saw people with no place to live. They were in pain, and they were **suffering**. Siddhartha wanted to know why there was so much suffering. He asked himself, "Can I help stop the suffering?"

Siddhartha left his home for a while. He lived outside by himself. He slept on the cold ground and did not have much to eat. But he found no answer. Then he began to practice a new way of thinking. He began to **meditate**. He wanted to understand how to stop suffering. He sat under a tree and meditated for 49 days.

LET'S TALK! Do you think meditating helped Siddhartha understand how to stop suffering?

palace place where a prince lives
suffering experiencing difficulty
mediate to be still and think deeply

5

He found an answer. It was like seeing a great light.
The answer was that people must not have **desires**. They
must stop wanting money or things. For the rest of his life,
Siddhartha taught this to others. He taught about life and
suffering. This became known as Buddhism. People called
him "Buddha."

---

desires strong wishes for things

What is Buddhism?

Have you ever tried to not want something? It is very hard to do. Buddha taught that people must not want money or **fame**. He taught that people would be happy if they didn't have desires. Later, they would reach happiness and **wisdom**. Wisdom is knowing how to live in the right way. Buddha said that wisdom ends suffering forever.

The main ideas of Buddhism seem simple. People must believe four truths. People must **follow** eight steps in order to live in the right way.

The Four Noble Truths

1. Life is full of suffering.

2. People suffer because they want worldly things.

3. The way to stop suffering is to stop this wanting.

4. The way to stop this wanting is to follow the Eightfold Path.

The Eightfold Path

1. Know and understand the Four Noble Truths.

2. Give up worldly things. Don't hate others.

3. Tell the truth. Don't talk about others behind their backs.

4. Don't do bad things like killing or stealing. Live a clean life.

5. Do work that matters.

6. Work for good. Work against evil.

7. Let your mind rule your senses.

8. Meditate.

fame being well known by many
wisdom deep understanding of many things
follow to be guided by something

Buddhism Today

Many people like the Buddha's message. His teachings give them hope for a happier and better life. Today around 350 million people follow the Eightfold Path. Buddhism helps people answer the same questions about life and suffering that Siddhartha Gautama asked long ago.

What Do You Think? Look back at the Eightfold Path. Which steps do you think are hard to follow? Which steps do you think are easy? Talk with a partner about them. Use the sentence frame below to get started.

I think that ___ is ___ to follow because ___.

Vocabulary for Mahatma Gandhi:

The Salt March Read the words and definitions below.

arrested (ə rest′ əd) *v.* The police have **arrested** a person when they think the person has broken a law.
Cognate (Spanish) **arrestar**

participate (pär ti′ sə pāt) *v.* When you **participate**, you join others who are doing something.
Cognate (Spanish) **participar**

disagreement (dis ə gre′ mənt) *n.* Two people have a **disagreement** when they argue or believe different things.

protests (prō′ tests) *n.* **Protests** are events when many people gather together to oppose something.
Cognate (Spanish) **protestas**

illegal (i lē′ gəl) *adj.* When you do not follow the law, you do something that is **illegal**.
Cognate (Spanish) **ilegal**

rule (rül) *n.* **Rule** is the power to make laws and have control over people.

inspired (in spīrd′) *v.* People are **inspired** when they see another person do a good or heroic act.
Cognate (Spanish) **inspirar**

tax (taks) *n.* A **tax** is money you have to pay to a government for goods and services.

Mahatma Gandhi
The Salt March

May 1, 1930

READ To Find Out — Why does Gandhi march?

Sabarmati, India—An Indian leader named Mahatma Gandhi is making news in India. Gandhi is upset with the British government. Gandhi feels the salt **tax** is unfair. He has been leading peaceful **protests**. He hopes to change the British law.

One protest began on March 12. Gandhi and 78 other people gathered to march. The march was a way to show **disagreement** with the salt tax. The people marched 248 miles from Sabarmati all the way to Dandi, near the ocean.

---

tax money collected by the government
protests large groups of people who gather to oppose something
disagreement different opinion

As the group walked, many other people joined them. The group walked for 23 days through many villages. More people joined the march every day. They finally reached the ocean on April 5th. There, Gandhi boiled some salty dirt to make his own salt. His simple act was a protest against British **rule**.

Now, thousands of Indians have been **inspired** to make their own salt. But British law says this is **illegal**. The police have **arrested** many people for making their own salt.

---

rule control over people
inspired influenced by someone
illegal against the law
arrested taken people to jail

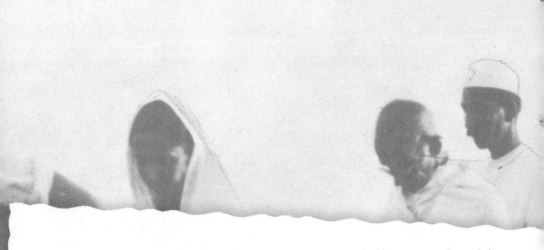

Some people say Gandhi and his followers should not **participate** in more protests. The British government says the protests are illegal. The government wants to keep **peace** in the country of India. They think that Gandhi and his protesters are not peaceful. They think Gandhi and his protesters should be punished.

It is clear that many people are not happy with the British government. They want to be free. They want to rule their own country. Will India gain more freedom from government control? Only the future will tell.

participate take part in
peace quiet or calm

What Do You Think? Read the following statement. Do you agree or disagree with it? Discuss your opinion in a small group.

People should not protest because they will be punished.

Friends to the Rescue

Literary Element Plot

The **plot** is what happens in a story.
Most plots have three parts.

> **conflict:** a problem that a character has
> **climax:** the turning point or main event
> **resolution:** how the story ends

As you read, think about parts of the plot. This will help you follow the order of events in a story.

Practice Read the paragraph. What happens first, second, and last?

One day, Amina left the front door open and her cat ran outside. She wanted him to come back in where it is safe. So she put food in his dish and called out his name. Quickly, the cat came inside again!

. . . .

Reading Strategy Visualize

When you visualize, you picture in your mind what is happening in the story. As you read, look for words that tell how things look, sound, smell, feel, and taste. These words can help you visualize the story.

As you read, complete the graphic organizer in the *Expressions Practice Book*.

Descriptive Detail	What I See in My Mind

Vocabulary for The King of Mazy May

Read the words and definitions below.

dragged (dragd') *v.* If you **dragged** something, you pulled it across the ground.

excitement (ik sīt' mənt) *n.* **Excitement** comes from feeling happy or looking forward to something.

fiercely (firs' lē) *adv.* When you do something with anger, you do it **fiercely**.

honest (ä' nəst) adj. Someone who is **honest** follows the rules.
Cognate (Spanish) **honesto(a)**

leader (lē' dər) n. A **leader** gives directions to a group.
Cognate (Spanish) **líder**

protecting (prə tekt' ing) v. If you are **protecting** something, you are keeping it safe from harm.
Cognate (Spanish) **proteger**

proud (praud') *adj.* When you feel **proud**, you are happy with yourself or others.

sled (sled') v. A **sled** is something you sit or stand on to slide over the snow.

The King of Mazy May

Based on a story
by Jack London

READ To Find Out — Who is Walt Masters?

Walt Masters can do many things that other boys do not know how to do. He can shoot a moose from very far away. He can drive a **sled** with wild wolf dogs many miles each day. Walt has a good heart and he is not afraid of being alone.

---

sled something to sit or stand on that slides on snow

When Walt's mother died, he and his father moved to Mazy May Creek. Walt and his father worked hard to find gold. At last, they found gold in the creek. But new people came to the area. They tried to **steal** land from many of the **honest** people who already lived there.

---

steal to take without asking
honest people who follow the law

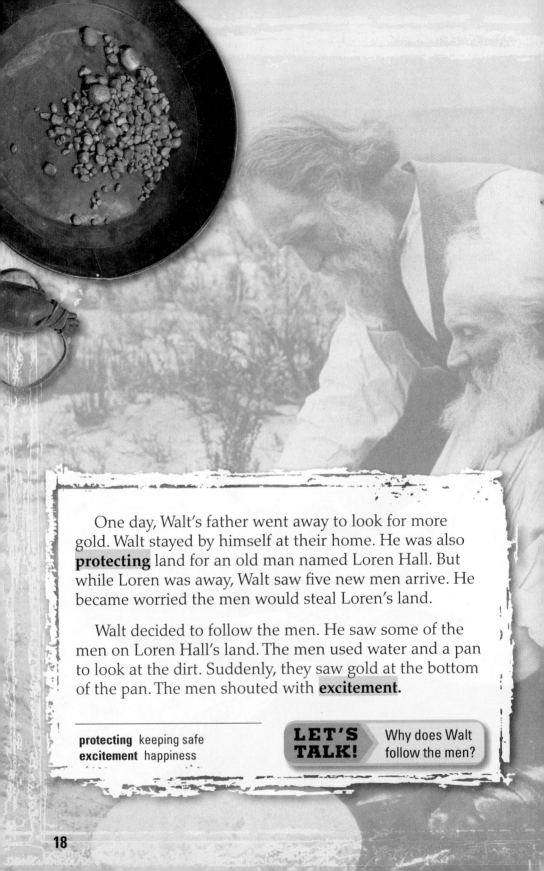

One day, Walt's father went away to look for more gold. Walt stayed by himself at their home. He was also **protecting** land for an old man named Loren Hall. But while Loren was away, Walt saw five new men arrive. He became worried the men would steal Loren's land.

Walt decided to follow the men. He saw some of the men on Loren Hall's land. The men used water and a pan to look at the dirt. Suddenly, they saw gold at the bottom of the pan. The men shouted with **excitement.**

protecting keeping safe
excitement happiness

LET'S TALK! Why does Walt follow the men?

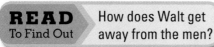

READ
To Find Out

How does Walt get away from the men?

Walt was only a boy, but he thought he should do something. He found the men's best sled. He took ten of their dogs. He tied the dogs to the sled and went to find Loren.

But the men saw Walt taking their sled and dogs. They yelled and ran after Walt. One man held on to the end of the sled. The dogs pulled the sled fast and **dragged** the man behind the sled. Walt hit the man over and over. Finally, the man let go and Walt got away.

---

dragged pulled

Walt drove the dogs along the **crooked** river. Three of the men had gotten other dogs and sleds. But two other men had run ahead and taken a shortcut. They had almost caught up to Walt!

Walt yelled at the dogs so they would run faster. The men shot at Walt, but the bullet missed him. The men could not keep running, so they waited for the other men on the sleds.

Walt soon knew he had chosen the wrong dog as the **leader**. The lead dog ran too close to the insides of the trail. The sled **tipped** over many times.

---

crooked not straight, twisting
leader dog that shows the others what to do
tipped fell

LET'S TALK! How does Walt feel while he is on the sled?

READ
To Find Out

Do the men catch Walt?

Walt could see the other sled behind him. He knew they were catching up to him. He was getting very tired.

Walt went over many hills. Each time the men came over a hill, they would shoot at him. Walt laid down on the sled while they shot. It was hard for the men to **aim** and shoot from a moving sled. Luckily, they missed Walt every time.

aim point at

Suddenly, a bullet hit the lead dog. The poor dog fell. The rest of the dogs piled on top of him. Walt looked back. The other sled was coming up fast! Walt jumped back onto the sled just as the men reached him.

Walt **fiercely attacked** the men with his whip. He hit their faces. They lifted their hands to protect themselves and couldn't shoot. Walt grabbed the legs of their lead dog. Their sled tipped over. The men were all **tangled** up.

---

fiercely violently; with a lot of force
attacked hit
tangled twisted together

Walt rode away. The best lead dog was now in front. The men were just a tiny **speck** behind Walt. He could no longer see them. Soon he found old Loren Hall.

---

speck small dot

Loren joined Walt on the sled. They went to the government office in Dawson to **report** what happened. And because of what Walt Masters did on this night, the men of the Yukon are very **proud** of him. They now call him the King of Mazy May.

report to make a complaint about
proud happy with

What Do You Think? How did Walt Masters help Loren Hall? Do you think Walt is a hero? Talk with a partner about what you think. Use the sentence frames below.

I think Walt is a hero because _____.

I don't think Walt is a hero because _____.

Larger Than Life

Prepare To Read

Literary Element Tone

Tone is how an author feels about a story. The tone can be sad, funny, or something else. To figure out the tone of a story

> ❯ think about the details that the author uses.
> ❯ look for clue words that show the tone.

Practice Read the paragraph. What is the tone of the paragraph? Which words are clues?

> The silly monkey danced on the tree branches. Then he threw an armful of coconuts at the zebras below. The zebras thought it was raining coconuts! The monkey laughed and laughed at the trick he played on the zebras.

Reading Skill Analyze Story Elements

Exaggeration is making something sound better or worse than it really is. You know you are reading a **tall tale** when the author uses exaggeration to describe characters, events, or settings. To **analyze story elements** in a tall tale, look for details that show what is real and what is exaggerated.

As you read, complete the graphic organizer in the *Expressions Practice Book*.

Larger-Than-Life Hero	Exaggeration	Humor

Vocabulary for Pecos Bill

Read the words and definitions below.

convinced (kən vinst') *v.* If someone **convinced** you, you believed what the person said.
Cognate (Spanish) **convencer**

recognized (re' kig nīzd) *v.* If someone **recognized** you, the person knew who you were.
Cognate (Spanish) **reconocer**

crowded (krau' dəd) *adj.* A place that is **crowded** has many people or buildings.

tamed (tāmd') *v.* When you have **tamed** a wild animal, the animal does what you want and will not harm you.

cyclone (sī' klōn) *n.* A **cyclone** is a storm with very strong winds.
Cognate (Spanish) **ciclón**

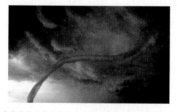

thirst (thərst') *n.* If your mouth is dry, you may have a **thirst** for water.

invented (in ven' təd) *v.* If someone created or made something new, the person **invented** it.
Cognate (Spanish) **inventar**

wagon (wa' gən) *n.* A **wagon** is a large cart with four wheels.

Pecos Bill

READ
To Find Out

What was Pecos Bill like
when he was young?

I bet you've heard about a lot of **cowboys.** Have you heard about Pecos Bill? No one anywhere can top him. He was the rip-snortingest, root-tootingest cowboy ever. I'm here to tell you the story of his life.

Baby Pecos Bill

Pecos Bill was born around 1830. He was the youngest child in a family with eighteen children. The family started out in West Texas. Then someone tried to start a **ranch** about 50 miles away. Bill's Ma said things were getting too **crowded**. So the family moved farther west.

As the **wagon** was crossing the Pecos River, baby Bill fell out of it. But, Bill was always a fast learner. He taught himself to swim right then. Well, sir, Bill lived!

---

cowboys workers on ranches who take care of horses
and cows
ranch a large farm
crowded too many people
wagon cart that is pulled by animals

Pecos Bill, the Cowboy

Then what? Bill sat in the sun. Just then, some **coyotes** came by. Those coyotes seemed to like Bill, so Bill followed them home. Pecos Bill then thought he was a coyote. That boy **ran on all fours** and **howled** at the moon.

One day Bill saw a cowboy who had stopped to let his horse drink water. The cowboy looked at Bill drinking water from the river just like a coyote. The cowboy kept looking at Bill. That boy was his little brother! The cowboy **recognized** Bill because Bill looked so much like their Ma.

Now the big brother decided to tell Bill that he was not really a coyote. At last, the big brother **convinced** the boy. Bill was happy about that. Now he could be a cowboy like his brother. And that is what Pecos Bill decided to do.

---

coyotes wild animals that look like dogs
ran on all fours used hands and knees to move quickly
howled made a long, loud, sad sound
recognized knew who he was
convinced made him believe

Remember, Pecos Bill was a fast learner. In just two days, he became the world's best cowboy. You could say he **invented** every good thing a cowboy can do.

Before Bill came along, cowboys could only run after **cattle.** They had to ride in front of the cattle to keep them in line. Then Bill had an idea. Bill fought the longest, biggest rattlesnake ever. He **tamed** that snake. He taught it to hold its tail in its mouth. The snake made a loop. Bill **squeezed** that snake so hard, it looked like rope. Pecos Bill invented the **lasso**! From then on, every cowboy used a lasso! Of course, only Bill used a snake. Everyone else used a rope. Then Bill decided a rope worked best, too.

LET'S TALK! What amazing things did Pecos Bill do?

invented created
cattle cows
tamed made the wild animal follow his orders
squeezed wrapped his arms around; hugged tightly
lasso a length of rope with a hoop at the end for catching cows

READ
To Find Out

How does Pecos Bill solve
a problem on his ranch?

A Big Ranch

Bill had a big ranch. How big was Bill's ranch? Well, the whole state of New Mexico could fit in his ranch. The weather was very dry there. One year the heat was so terrible that Bill's ranch was dry as dust. Pecos Bill would not sit still while his ranch dried up and his cattle died of **thirst**. No, sir. Bill started to dig. Soon he dug a whole river. The water flowed right to his ranch. Now we call that river the Rio Grande.

---

thirst needing something to drink

31

Bill Rides On

Bill could ride anything that walked, swam, or flew. Once, he threw his lasso and caught a mountain lion. That lion wasn't an ordinary little lion. It was as big as a buffalo. It took Bill almost three hours to put a **saddle** on that lion. Then he rode that lion like a horse.

One day, Bill was riding the lion, when saw the most dangerous horse ever. He knew that horse. It was Widow-Maker. It got that name for a simple reason. It killed every man who ever tried to ride it. Bill tamed **Widow**-Maker in about twenty minutes. They were good friends from that moment on.

---

saddle a seat on a horse or other animal so that people can ride it
widow a woman whose husband has died

> **LET'S TALK!** How did Pecos Bill find his horse?

32

Pecos Bill in Bad Weather

One day, Bill was with the cattle on his ranch. A great storm started. It was a **cyclone**! You've seen little balls of **hail** fall from the sky. Well, this hail was a big as **boulders**! The winds blew very hard. When the cyclone was still three miles away, half of the cattle blew away. That's how strong that wind was. Bill could see the cyclone was going **to wipe out** most of Texas. He figured it would destroy all of Kansas, too. He decided to put a stop to it.

Pecos Bill threw his lasso over that cyclone. He stopped it by digging his heels into the ground. Then he grabbed that cyclone and pulled it down to the ground. He jumped on its back and tried to ride it just like a horse.

---

cyclone a tornado; spinning winds that form a funnel
hail pieces of frozen rain
boulders very large rocks
to wipe out to destroy

The cyclone twisted harder than the angriest wild horse. Bill just laughed and waved his hat. He kicked the cyclone's sides to make it go faster. This was the most fun Pecos Bill had ever had.

Finally, the cyclone **gave up**. It stopped spinning. The wind stopped blowing. The hail stopped falling. Pecos Bill squeezed the rain out of the giant cyclone. Then the rain poured down hard. All that rain formed the Grand Canyon!

---

gave up stopped

What Do You Think? The exaggeration in tall tales is fun to read and imagine. Talk with a partner about exaggeration that you use. Describe food, animals, the weather, or something else. Make a list of your exaggerations. Start with these examples.

The hail is as big as boulders.

The ___ is as ___ as ___.

Young and Brave

Talk About It!

What does it mean
to be brave?

READ
- Nkosi Johnson: A Boy Like a King
- "A Man"

Literary Element Theme

The **theme** is the main idea, or message, of a story or poem.

> Sometimes an author clearly tells readers what the theme is. This is a **stated theme**.

> Sometimes readers must find clues to help them know the theme. This is an **implied theme**.

As you read, use titles and subheads to help you understand the theme of the text.

Reading Skill Compare and Contrast Theme

You can compare and contrast texts that you read. You can think about ways they are alike or different. This helps you understand each text better. As you read the texts, **compare and contrast themes** for each one.

> What is the main idea, or theme, of each text?

> How are the themes of each text alike?

> How are the themes of each text different?

As you read, complete the graphic organizer in the *Expressions Practice Book*.

Title	Subject	Speaker	Admired Quality

Vocabulary   for Nkosi Johnson: A Boy Like a King

Read the words and definitions below.

awareness (ə wer′ nəs) *n.*
Awareness is knowing about something.

bleed (blēd′) *v.* When you get cut and lose blood, you **bleed**.

courageous (kə rā′ jəs) *adj.* If you bravely face your fears, you are **courageous**.

disclose (dis klōz′) *v.* When you **disclose** something, you let other people know about it.

discriminated (dis kri′ mə nā təd) *v.* When people are not treated fairly because of who they are, they are **discriminated** against.
Cognate (Spanish) **discriminar**

disease (di zēz′) *n.* A **disease** is an illness in the body.

honor (ä′ nər) *v.* When you **honor** a person, you point out ways that person is important or special.
Cognate (Spanish) **honor**

infected (in fek′ təd) *v.* When you get sick, germs have **infected** your body.
Cognate (Spanish) **infectada**

Nkosi Johnson:
A Boy Like a King

READ To Find Out | Who is Nkosi Johnson?

"**C**are for us and accept us. We are all human beings. We are normal. We have hands. We have feet. We can walk, we can talk. We have needs just like everyone else. Don't be afraid of us. We are all the same!"

An eleven-year-old boy from South Africa named Nkosi Johnson gave this speech. Nkosi had Acquired Immune Deficiency Syndrome (AIDS). AIDS is a **disease** that has killed millions of people. Nkosi fought for the rights of children with the same disease until his death in 2001. This is his **courageous** story.

---

disease sickness
courageous bravely facing fears

A Baby Is Born

Daphne Nkosi was **infected** with HIV. On February 4, 1989, she had a baby boy she named Xolani Nkosi. Her newborn son was also infected.

When Nkosi was two years old, he and his mother were living in a care center for people with HIV/AIDS. Daphne was becoming too sick to care for her son. Gail Johnson was in charge of running the center. Gail wanted to help Daphne. Daphne agreed to let Gail become Nkosi's foster mother.

Gail knew babies with AIDS **rarely** lived past the age of two. So Gail believed Nkosi would only live a few more months.

infected sick
rarely almost never

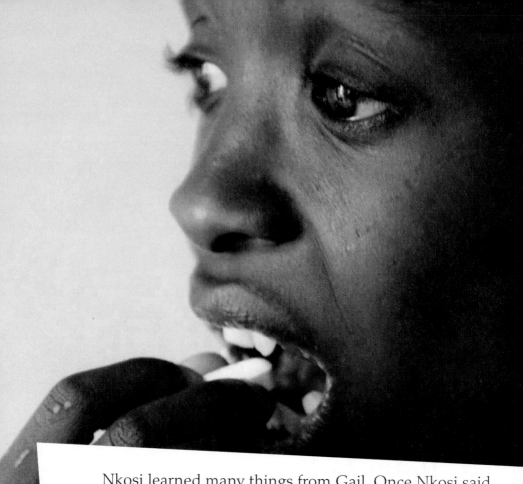

Nkosi learned many things from Gail. Once Nkosi said, "She has taught me all about being infected and how I must be careful with my blood... I know that my blood is only dangerous to other people if they also have an open **wound** and my blood goes into it." Gail taught Nkosi what to do if he ever got a cut and started to **bleed**. First, Nkosi needed to cover the cut. Then, he had to ask an adult to help clean the cut.

The Right to Go to School

When Gail first sent Nkosi to school, she had to **disclose** that Nkosi had AIDS. Many parents didn't want Nkosi to go to the school. They were afraid that he would infect their children.

wound break in the skin
bleed to lose or leak blood
disclose let others know

LET'S TALK! What did Gail do to help Nkosi?

The school set up AIDS **awareness** meetings. Students, parents, and teachers learned more about the disease. Because of the meetings, the school let Nkosi become a student. Today, children with AIDS cannot be **discriminated** against. They can **attend** school like everyone else.

AIDS Awareness

Gail and Nkosi traveled the world to talk about AIDS awareness. In July, 2000, Nkosi gave a speech at the International AIDS Conference in Durban, South Africa. Wearing a new black suit and sneakers, he spoke in front of 10,000 people. People all over the world watched him on television.

In his speech, Nkosi said, "When I grow up, I want to talk to more and more people about AIDS. You can't get AIDS if you touch, hug, kiss, or hold hands with someone who is infected."

---

awareness information
discriminated treated unfairly
attend go to

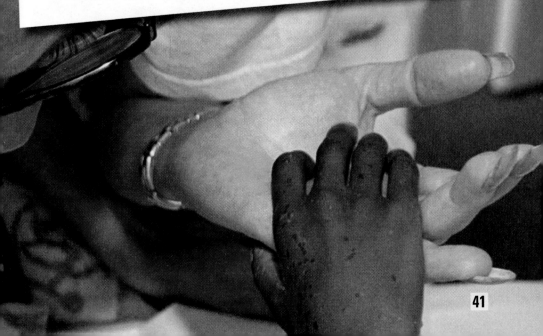

41

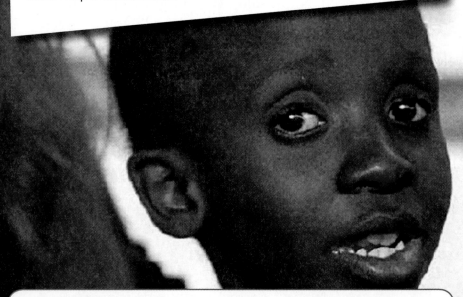

Still Helping People

On June 9, 2001, Nkosi died. He was only twelve years old, but he helped many people during his life. He had a message to share.

"Do all you can do with what you have," he said.

Gail wanted to do something important in memory of her son. She started "Nkosi's **Haven**" to **honor** him. Women and children who have the disease can go to Nkosi's Haven to get medicine and other help.

In the Zulu language, Nkosi means "king of kings." This courageous boy proved that he was a "king of kings."

---

haven safe place
honor help others remember

What Do You Think? Do you know a courageous person? Talk with a partner about the person. Use the sentence frames below.

The courageous person I know is ___.

This person is courageous because ___.

Vocabulary for "A Man"

Read the words and definitions below.

applaud (ə plôd') *v.* You **applaud** when you clap your hands to show you like something.
Cognate (Spanish) **aplaudir**

bang (bang') *v.* When you **bang** on something, you hit it and cause a loud noise.

country (kən' trē) *n.* A **country** is the area of land under the control of one government.

fighting (fīt' əng) *v.* You are **fighting** when you take part in a battle or war.

half (haf') *n.* A **half** is one of two equal parts. Two halves make a whole.

lost (lôst') *v.* When you cannot find a thing, you have **lost** it.

torn (torn') *v.* When something is pulled apart by force, it has been **torn**.

wing (wing') *n.* The part of a bird that looks like an arm is a **wing**. Birds use their wings to fly.

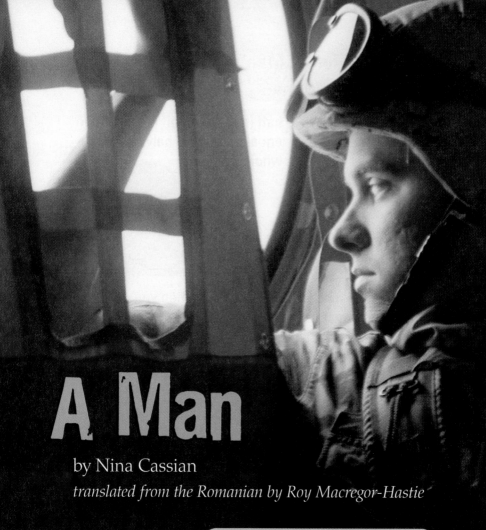

A Man

by Nina Cassian

translated from the Romanian by Roy Macregor-Hastie

READ
To Find Out
What problem does the man have?

While **fighting** for his **country**, he **lost** an arm and was suddenly afraid:

"From now on, I shall only be able to **do things by halves**.

fighting going into battle
country land he was born in
lost no longer has
do things by halves doing only part of a job

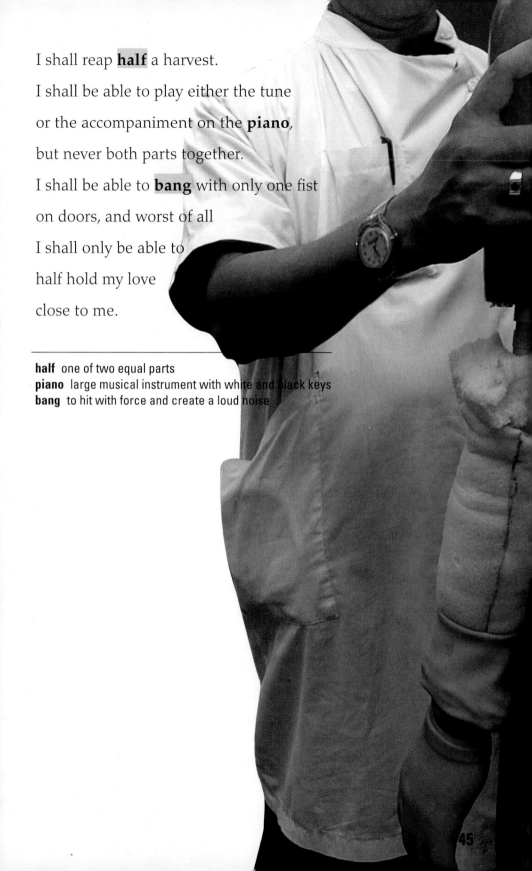

I shall reap **half** a harvest.

I shall be able to play either the tune

or the accompaniment on the **piano**,

but never both parts together.

I shall be able to **bang** with only one fist

on doors, and worst of all

I shall only be able to

half hold my love

close to me.

---

half one of two equal parts
piano large musical instrument with white and black keys
bang to hit with force and create a loud noise

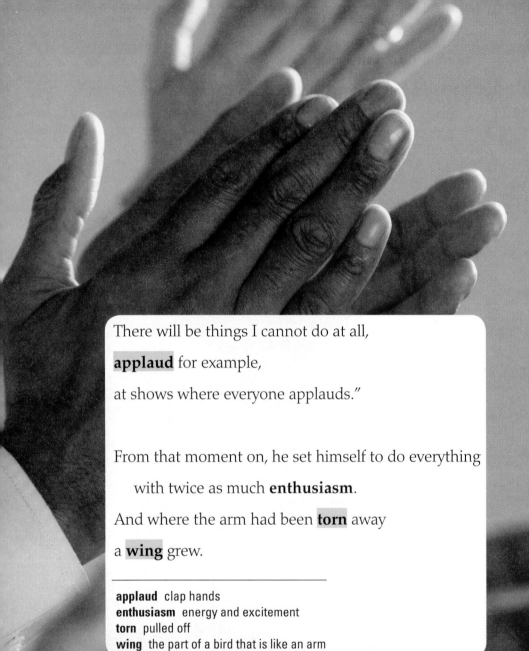

There will be things I cannot do at all,

applaud for example,

at shows where everyone applauds."

From that moment on, he set himself to do everything

with twice as much **enthusiasm**.

And where the arm had been **torn** away

a **wing** grew.

---

applaud clap hands
enthusiasm energy and excitement
torn pulled off
wing the part of a bird that is like an arm

What Do You Think? The word *wing* means different things to different people. With a partner, think of as many ideas that connect to *wing* as you can. Make a list and share your ideas with others.

▣ Writing Workshop

Writing a Narrative

Writing That Tells a Story
A **narrative** tells a story. Think about how you tell a story to a friend. You explain the plot, or what happened. You describe the characters, or the people or animals, in the story. You also describe the setting, or where the story takes place.

Writing Assignment
For this Writing Workshop, you will write a **short story** about a hero. One way to be a hero is to keep trying when a goal is difficult. You will write your story for your classmates and your teacher. They will be your audience.

WRITING PLAN

> Think of a plot for your short story. The plot must include a conflict and the solution.

> Choose a narrator and a point of view.

> Include sensory details to describe the setting and the action.

> Use dialogue and description to show how characters are alike and different.

Writing Model
Read the student model below.

> A crowd of students read the flyer in the school hallway. They all talked at once.
> "It's the school talent show!" said a student.
> Lin smiled. "My band is fantastic! The drummer is the best in the whole school. We'll take first prize," she said proudly.
> Anna frowned. "I know I'm the best drummer," she thought to herself.
> Anna also knew something else. She wasn't in a band.

1. Think of Story Ideas

To get started on your short story, think about hero stories that you know. Brainstorm about the hero story you will write. Ask yourself: What is a good setting? What will the characters be like? What is the conflict? Write your ideas in a chart.

Setting	Characters	Conflict
school, today	middle school kids	They can't be in a talent show.

2. Choose a Point of View

Every story has a **narrator** who tells the story. The reader "sees" the story from the narrator's point of view. Choose the point of view that will work best with your story.

- **First-person point of view** uses a narrator who is a character in the story. The character uses pronouns such as *I* and *we* to tell what happens.

- **Third-person point of view** uses a narrator who is outside the story. This narrator uses pronouns such as *he, she, it,* and *they* to tell what happens.

3. Organize the Story

Use a story map to plan your story.

Setting: school, present time
Characters: Anna, Lin, Mr. Turner

Conflict: Anna wants to be in the talent show, but she isn't in a band.

Beginning What happens first?	Middle What happens in the middle?	End What happens last?
Anna and Lin see a flyer for a talent show.	1. Lin searches for a drummer. 2. Anna tries out for Lin's band. 3. Lin asks Anna to join her band.	Lin's band performs and wins a third place ribbon.

Draft

1. Start Writing

Use your story map to help you write your story.

2. Add to Your Draft

Use **dialogue** in your short story. Dialogue is what the character says.

> "I practice more than anyone I know," said Anna.

> Lin said, "Only the best player can be in my band."

Use **sensory details**. These details connect to what you see, hear, touch, and smell.

> The students roared and clapped.

> The drumsticks were a blur as Anna played.

USE GOOD WRITING TRAITS: ORGANIZATION

Organization is the order of events in a story. Good organization helps readers understand the story.

Sometimes writers organize stories by time. **Time order words** tell when things happen. Read the sentences below. Pay attention to the words that help you understand the order of events.

> **Now,** Anna and Lin stared at the flyer about the talent show.

> **Right** away, they both decided to perform.

> **Then,** Anna groaned. How could she join a band quickly?

As you write your story, remember to choose words that show the order of events in your story.

Revise

Now it's time to revise your draft. This step helps you make
your writing better, so that others will want to read it.

1. **Read Your Story** Ask yourself these questions:
   - Does it have a strong beginning? Does the middle show the
     conflict? Does the end solve the problem?
   - Which sensory details did you use?
   - Is there a variety of long and short sentences?
   - Does the dialogue make the characters seem real?

2. **Show Your Story** Trade drafts with a partner. Answer these
   questions as you read your partner's story.
   - Do I know the narrator's point of view?
   - Is the conflict part of every event?
   - Is the story interesting?

3. **Make Your Changes** Talk with your partner to help you decide
   what changes you need to make. Then revise your draft.

> **Technology** Use the design features of your word
> processing software to add or create graphics that will bring out
> the details of your story. Make your text look better by making
> your margins wider or narrower. When you add a title, use a
> font that matches the tone of your writing.

Edit and Proofread

1. **Proofread Your Story** Reread your story. Look for mistakes in capitalization, punctuation, or spelling. Use the proofreading symbols in the chart on page 353 to mark changes.

2. **Check Your Sentences** Did you use complete sentences? Do subjects and verbs agree? Make changes if you need to.

Grammar Focus: Punctuation of Dialogue

Remember to use quotation marks for dialogue. Look at the examples to see how to fix problems.

The Problem: It is unclear which words the speaker says.

I must find out a way to perform! Anna said to herself.

The Solution: Place quotation marks before and after the spoken words.

"I must find a way to perform," Anna said to herself.

The Problem: Punctuation is incorrect in the quotation.

"Show up at 6 o'clock sharp, Anna, she ordered."

The Solution: Put a comma and a quotation mark at the end of the spoken words. Then add the speaker tag and a period.

"Show up at 6 o'clock sharp, Anna," she ordered.

3. **Make a Final Copy** Make the corrections that you marked. If you are working on the computer, print out the corrected work. If not, rewrite it.

Present

Here are some ways to share your writing.

- Add pictures to your story. Give it to your friends to read and ask them for their comments.
- Act out your story as a play. Choose students to take the parts of the narrator and the characters.

🔖 Speaking, Listening, and Viewing Workshop

Narrative Presentation

Activity

1. Connect to Your Writing
Give an oral presentation of a short story narrative to your classmates. Use the short story you wrote for the Writing Workshop on pages 47-51.

2. Plan Your Presentation
Reread your story. Mark the parts that you want to include in your presentation. Remember that the plot has a beginning, a middle, and an end. Write the important events, dialogue, and descriptive details on note cards.

3. Practice Your Presentation
Practice your presentation in front of a mirror. Watch your facial expressions and gestures. Listen to the volume and style of your voice. Practice your narrative until you feel ready to give your presentation.

4. Give Your Presentation
- Speak clearly.
- Say the dialogue the way the characters would speak.
- Speed up or slow down to tell important events.
- Change how soft or loud you speak to show emotions and suspense.

LISTENING TO APPRECIATE
As you listen to another student's presentation, take notes. What did you like about the story? Why did you enjoy the way the student presented it? Share your ideas with the student. Use the sentence frames below.

- I liked how you moved when you spoke because ____ .
- I could picture the story because ____ .
- The character I liked best was ____ because ____.

How to Get Things Done

Talk About It!

Why do you need to know how to fill out a form?

READ
- Mail Order Form
- Library Card Application Form
- Membership Application

53

Prepare To Read

Skim and Scan

When you **skim** a text, you read it quickly.
Skimming helps you find the most important
ideas in a text. As you read,

> look at text features, like titles, heads,
> subheads, and charts.

> look at the text structure:
> Is it compare and contrast, time order,
> or something else?

When you **scan** a text, you look for words
and phrases that help you find information
or details. As you read,

> look for important words.

> look for important phrases.

Try It! Think about how to skim and scan a text. Then with a partner
answer the questions below.

1. Skim the text below. What is it about?

2. When does Coach Van's team practice? Scan to find the correct day
   and time.

3. Would you skim or scan to find out if soccer practice is on Monday?

Bay County Sports Practice Schedule		
Team Coach	**Day**	**Time**
Girls' Basketball		
Coach Sharif	Monday	5:00-6:00
Coach Collins	Tuesday	9:00-10:30
Coach Washington	Thursday	8:00-9:00
Coach Turner	Thursday	9:00-10:30
Boys' Basketball		
Coach Vargas	Tuesday	4:00-6:00
Coach Cole	Friday	6:00-8:00
Coach Van	Tuesday	6:00-800
Coach Miller	Friday	8:00-10:00
Girls' Soccer		
Coach Rashid	Monday	4:00-5:00
Coach O'Donnell	Friday	3:30-6:00
Boys' Soccer		
Coach Martinez	Monday	7:00-8:30
Coach Woo	Monday	8:30-10:00

Vocabulary for Mail Order Form; Library Card Application Form; Membership Form

Read the words and definitions below.

application (a plə kā' shən) *n.* One form that people and businesses use is an **application**.

bill (bil') *v.* A store will **bill** you because you bought something and you must pay for it.

guardian (gär' dē ən) *n.* Someone who takes care of another person is a **guardian**.

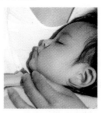

identification (ī den tə fə kā' shən) *n.* **Identification** is proof of who someone is.

instructions (in strək' shənz) *n.* **Instructions** are a list of steps that tell you how to do or make something.

Cognate (Spanish) **instrucciones**

magazine (ma' gə zēn') *n.* A **magazine** is a printed booklet that has stories and articles.

membership (mem' bər ship) *n.* When you have a **membership**, you are officially in a club or a group.

print (print') *v.* To **print** is to write in letters like the ones you see in this sentence.

Mail Order Form

SCIENCE KID

A **magazine** *for* children interested in *science*

☐ *4* issues *for $15.97*   ☐ *12* issues *for $30.00*

Child's Name (please **print**)_____

Address _____

City/State/Zip_____

Bill to: _____

Adult's Name _____

Address _____

City/State/Zip_____

Please allow 4–6 weeks for delivery.

_____

magazine publication that has stories or articles
print to write letters like the ones you see in this sentence
bill send a letter to ask for money

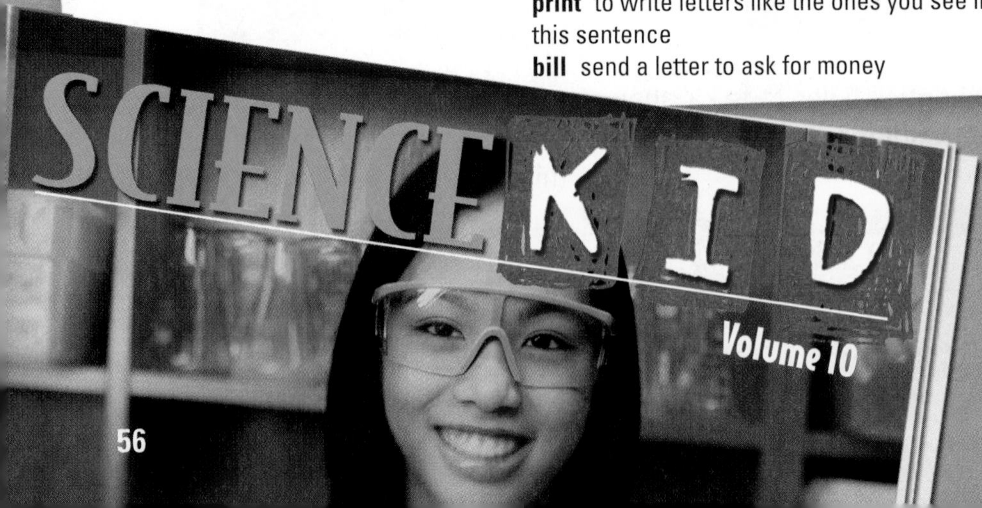

SCIENCE KID

Volume 10

UNITED STATES POSTAGE

HONORING THOSE
WHO HAVE SERVED

Return your order form to
Science Kid Magazine
634 East Hillside Avenue
Rogers, CA 12345

What Do You Think? Talk about other forms that you will have to fill out. Discuss the information you will need to fill out those forms. Use the sentence frame below.

To fill out forms you need ___.

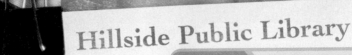

Hillside Public Library

READ To Find Out — How do you fill out a form to get a library card?

Instructions: Please complete this **application** form and turn it in to the front desk. A parent or **guardian** must show **identification** with this form. The library card will be ready the next business day.

Date _____

Name of Child _____

Date of Birth _____

Address (street, city) _____

Name of Parent/Guardian _____

Address _____

Phone _____

E-mail Address _____

Password Number for Online Library Web Site _____

Parent/Guardian: Please read the information below. Check the first box. Then, check any other boxes to let us know how your child may use his/her card.

☐ I agree to pay for or replace lost, late, or damaged materials checked out by this cardholder.

☐ I agree to let this cardholder use the Internet.

☐ I do not agree to let this cardholder use the Internet.

---

instructions steps that tell you how to do something
application a form you complete before joining a group
guardian person who is responsible for someone else
identification form or card that proves who you are

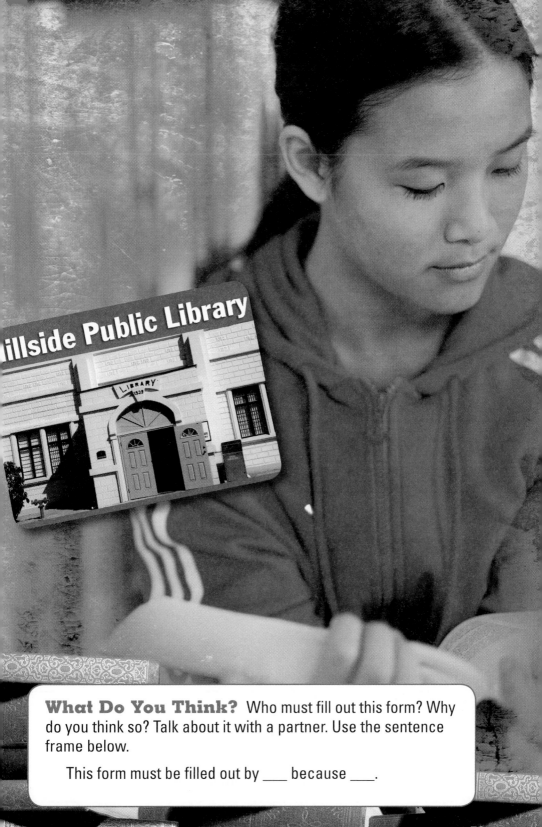

What Do You Think? Who must fill out this form? Why do you think so? Talk about it with a partner. Use the sentence frame below.

This form must be filled out by ___ because ___.

Membership Application

THE Backyard Explorer CLUB

Yes! I want to be a member of the Backyard Explorers Club.

☐ **Enclosed is my yearly membership fee of $10.**
Form of Payment: ○ check   ○ money order
☐ **Please send me a bill for my membership fee of $10.**

Name _____

Date of Birth _____

Address _____

Phone _____

E-mail Address of Parent/Guardian

_____

☐ Please send me information about how to earn
Backyard Explorers books and games.

Send to:
Backyard Explorers Club, 111 Smith Ave., Cary, IL 60013

For Office Use Only:
Member Number_____Membership Paid_____
Send Book/Game Info_____

_____

membership belonging to a group

> **What Do You Think?** What is the most important
> information on the form? Talk with a partner. Use the sentence
> frame below.
>
>   I think the most important information is___ because ___.

To Build
a Great Country

Talk About It!

What makes a leader powerful?

READ • A Silent Army of Clay

Literary Element Description

Authors use **description** to give the reader
details about a person, a thing, or an event.
Descriptive writing helps readers see, hear,
smell, taste, and feel the details in a text.
Descriptive writing also helps readers make
connections with the characters in a story.
As you read:

> ❯ look for words and phrases about seeing, hearing, smelling, tasting, and touching.

> ❯ use the words and phrases to visualize what is happening in the text.

Reading Skill Recognize Author's Purpose

Author's purpose is the reason the author has for writing. An
author may want to entertain or inform readers. An author may
even want to persuade readers to think about something in a new
way. An author also may have more than one purpose. When you
recognize author's purpose, you understand why the text was
written. As you read, look for main ideas and supporting details.
Then think about what you learn from reading the text.
As you read, complete the graphic organizer in the *Expressions
Practice Book*.

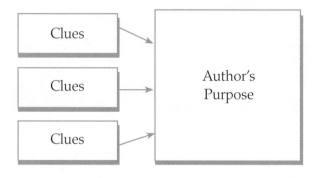

Vocabulary for A Silent Army of Clay

Read the words and definitions below.

archeologists (är kē′ ä lə jists) *n.* **Archeologists** study fossils and ancient objects.
Cognate (Spanish) **arqueólogos**

ferocious (fə rō′ shəs) *adj.* Something that is very mean and violent is **ferocious**.
Cognate (Spanish) **feroz**

conquered (käng′ kərd) *v.* When one army has won the war, that army **conquered** the enemy.
Cognate (Spanish) **conquistar**

kingdoms (king′ dəmz) *n.* **Kingdoms** are regions that are ruled by kings or queens.

dynasty (dī′ nə stē) *n.* A **dynasty** is a series of rulers from the same family. Cognate (Spanish) **dinastía**

potion (pō′ shən) n. A **potion** is a mixture of liquids to make medicine. Cognate (Spanish) **poción**

emperor (em′ pər ər) *n.* An **emperor** is a male ruler of an empire. Cognate (Spanish) **emperador**

tomb (tüm′) n. A **tomb** is a house or chamber that holds the dead.
Cognate (Spanish) **tumba**

A Silent Army of Clay

READ
To Find Out

Who was
Emperor Qin?

Imagine being the ruler of a large country as a teenager. What would you do with your **power**? Would you be **worried** that someone might want to take your place as king?

Qin (chin) became the first **emperor** of China when he was thirteen years old. However, he felt danger all around, and worried about losing his position. Qin made sure everyone did what he said. If a person did not obey Qin, the ruler gave the person a heavy **punishment**. Sometimes the punishment was death.

---

power control over others
worried afraid, nervous
emperor male ruler
punishment negative action done as a response to behavior

When Qin became emperor, China had seven kingdoms. These **kingdoms** were always fighting each other in wars. Qin fought the other kingdoms for nine years. Over one million people died in these wars.

Finally, Qin **conquered** the other six kingdoms. Now, Qin was the highest ruler. He made all the kingdoms one great empire and ruled over it. After Emperor Qin died, his family ruled for many years. This line of Qin rulers was the Qin **Dynasty**.

The Great Builder

At first, the kingdoms in the empire had different laws and their people spoke different languages. They also used different types of money. Qin used his power to make the kingdoms more alike. Emperor Qin wanted only one large **government**. He wanted everyone to speak one language and use one writing **system**. Also, everyone would use the same money. These were great changes.

---

kingdoms lands ruled by kings or queens
conquered won a war against
dynasty line of rulers from one family
government a way of managing a country or an area
system an ordered set of things

Qin used his great power to make his empire better. Yet this emperor had **complete control** of his people. He did not let anyone question him. Once, a group of people told Qin that China should no longer be an empire. Qin became very angry. To show his power, he ordered his soldiers to kill 460 people.

Emperor Qin showed his power in other ways too. He **ordered** his workers to build the Great Wall of China. The Great Wall is many thousands of miles long.

Builders also made more than 700 palaces for the Emperor in all parts of China. Workers also built wide, straight roads for the emperor and his armies to use.

> **LET'S TALK!** How did Emperor Qin build his empire?

---

complete control power to make anyone do anything
ordered told people what to do

To Live Forever

Qin believed that he would never die. He thought that he would find a magic **potion** to make him live forever. He traveled the empire searching for the potion, but he never found it. Qin died at the age of 49.

However, Qin **prepared** for his death. He started work on his **tomb** when he became emperor at age thirteen. At one time, he had 700,000 people working to build it.

After Qin died, the next rulers of the empire decided to keep the tomb secret. So, many artists and other workers who built the tomb had to die too. They were buried alive with the emperor.

Qin believed that after he died, he would need the same things that he had in his life. So he wanted an army to protect him. Workers built an army from **clay**. The clay army was buried in the tomb.

---

potion mixture of liquids to make medicine
prepared got ready for
tomb a room for a dead body
clay sticky mud that can be shaped

The tomb stayed secret for many hundreds of years. Then, some Chinese farmers digging in a field found the clay soldiers. This was the clay army that was buried with Emperor Qin.

Archaeologists have found almost 7,500 clay soldiers dressed for battle. When visitors see thousands of the life-like soldiers in one place, they agree that they are an amazing sight.

archaeologists people who study fossils

It is more amazing to see that each face is different. They have different eyes, noses, and mouths. They even have different **expressions**. Some soldiers look **ferocious**. Some look serious. And some look peaceful. Archaeologists say that the faces of the soldiers may be the faces of those who made them. Imagine making a face that people would find over 2,000 years later.

The Emperor Qin was powerful and sometimes mean. Today, people come from all over the world to see what he built. They admire the Great Wall of China and the clay soldiers. They also **admire** his imagination and ideas for building a great country.

---

expressions looks that show feelings
ferocious mean
admire to think highly of

What Do You Think? Imagine you could go back in time to meet Emperor Qin. What questions would you ask him? With a partner, take turns being Emperor Qin and a person from today. Then ask and answer questions.

Power of the Sun

Talk About It!

Why is the sun so important to the Earth?

READ
- The Sand Castle
- Heating with Sunlight

Prepare To Read

Literary Element Mood

Read about **mood** below. Then read the paragraph. What is the mood of the paragraph?

> Mood is the emotion or feeling of a story.

> Details about setting, or other parts of a text, can create a mood that is happy, sad, or something else.

> Look for words that are clues about the mood of a story. For example, "bright sunshine" is a detail that creates a happy mood.

Juan stood outside the door of the music room. His heart was beating very fast. His mouth felt dry. Juan had worked so hard to learn his song. Now, he was about to sing it for Miss Sims. Would she like his singing enough to put him in the play? Juan took a deep breath and walked in.

Reading Strategy Connect to Today

When you **connect to today**, you link what you are reading to real life. Connecting to today helps you understand the writer's message.

As you read, complete the graphic organizer in the *Expressions Practice Book*.

Issue in Story	Issue Today

Vocabulary for The Sand Castle

Read the words and definitions below.

dangerous (dān′ jə rəs) *adj.* Something is **dangerous** when it is unsafe or could hurt someone.

remember (ri mem′ bər) *v.* When you **remember**, you think of something again.

decorate (de′ kə rāt) *v.* When you **decorate** something, you make it look prettier or more interesting.

seashells (sē′ shelz) *n.* **Seashells** are the hard outer coverings some sea animals leave behind.

goggles (gä′ gəlz) *n.* **Goggles** are glasses that protect your eyes.

toxic (täk′ sik) *adj.* If you get sick after eating or drinking something, you had something that was **toxic**.
Cognate (Spanish) **tóxico**

protective (prə tek′ tiv) *adj.* To be **protective** is to guard from something that could hurt or harm.

waves (wāvz′) *n.* Wind makes **waves** when it moves water.

The Sand Castle

**Based on a story
by Alma Luz Villanueva**

READ
To Find Out — What was it like when
Masha was a child?

"Are you dressed?" Masha called. "My poor grandchildren," she sighed to herself. "They don't **remember** when the sun warmed the land **gently**. They don't know what it feels like to play in the sea. Maybe, one day the sun will not burn so hotly and the sea will welcome people and sea animals again."

Masha put on the **goggles** and thick gloves, so different from when she was a child. She remembered her mother saying, "Masha, put your bathing suit on under your clothes. Hurry, Father is waiting!" She remembered the bus rides to the shore and the first time she walked on the beach. She felt the sand between her toes.

---

remember to think of something again
gently mildly; not too much
goggles something to wear over the eyes to protect them

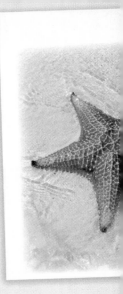

Her father liked to swim out as far as he could, and back. Then, he would lie in the warm sun.

Masha liked to lie on the wet sand and feel the **waves** flow over her. At that time, she never **noticed** the sun. It was just there, light and warm. She only thought of the sea. The cool, blue water was wonderful. Fish and other sea animals swam below, and the beach was full of birds and people.

Masha remembered building sand castles with her father. She would find the **seashells** to **decorate** them. Her father would say, "The Princess's castle is ready for the Prince!"

LET'S TALK! What was it like to go to the sea when Masha was a child?

---

waves moving water
noticed to see or be aware of
seashells hard coverings no longer needed by sea animals
decorate to make pretty

Her mother would say, "It is fit for a Queen! Can I live in your castle, Princess Masha?"

"Of course," Masha would reply. "You can live with me always...."

She remembered her mother's beautiful red hair shining in the sun.

The sun, the sun, the sun. Everyone noticed the small changes. Winters came later each year, and spring flowers **bloomed** earlier. But, few people believed life would change. Then, the **temperature** began to rise, and the sea life started to die. Scientists searched for answers, but the damage was done. Maybe, thought Masha, her great grandchildren would feel the sun on their skin and play in the sea.

Now, most people went outside only at night. Anyone outside in the daytime wore **protective** clothing.

---

bloomed to become flowers
temperature measurement of heat or cold
protective guard from something that could hurt or harm

Masha missed having the sunlight shine through her windows. She missed the birds, too.

But today, Masha was taking her grandchildren to the sea. She knew they hated the protective clothes. Never mind, she told herself. They can take off the gloves and goggles in the bus.

Masha and her grandchildren had been to the sea before. They sat, playing with the sand, looking **bored**. Masha told them stories of her father swimming. To her grandchildren though, the sea was just black, **toxic** liquid they could not touch or drink. It was **dangerous**, like the sun.

But today, Masha had a secret. Today she and her grandchildren would build a sand castle. She packed everything they needed.

LET'S TALK! How do the children prepare to go to the sea?

---

bored not interested
toxic poison
dangerous something that hurts people

Masha hoped it would help her remember the happiness of her childhood. She hoped it would help her remember the cool blue sea that she knew as a child.

The bus stopped. Masha and her grandchildren walked slowly across the sand toward the dark water. "We're going to build a sand castle today," Masha said with a smile.

"What's that?" the boy asked.

"You'll see. I'll show you."

"Is it fun, Grandmama?" the girl smiled and took Masha's hand.

"Yes, it's so much fun. You'll see!"

The boy jumped. "Show us, Grandmama!"

Together Masha and her grandchildren set to work. The children were so excited they forgot about their gloves. They rushed back and forth, bringing the wet, dark sand. Their eyes were happy behind their goggles.

"A little wet sand won't hurt. Just don't get your gloves in the water,"Masha told them."When I was a girl there were so many birds at the sea. Seagulls, they were, big white birds that liked to scream at the sea, they sounded like eagles to me…"

"What are eagles, Grandmama?" the boy asked.

"They used to be one of the largest, most beautiful birds in the world."

Remembering the past made her sad.

This is no time for sadness, Masha told herself. The sand castle is what is important now.

"I have a wonderful **surprise**," she said.

"Show us, Grandmama, please?" said the boy

Masha took eight seashells out of a bag: eight shells from all over the world.

"But Grandmama," **exclaimed** the girl."Those are your special shells! You said the sea doesn't make them anymore…."

"Someday it will again, Anna."Masha hugged her granddaughter."Today we decorate our sand castle with these, yes!"

---

surprise something that is not expected
exclaimed to say as if surprised

What Do You Think? In this story, Masha feels it is important for her grandchildren to learn about the past. Why is it important for people to learn about the past? Discuss your answers with a group. Use the sentence frame below to write your answer.

It is important to learn about the past because _____.

Vocabulary for Heating with Sunlight

Read the words and definitions below.

absorbed (əb sorbd') *v.* Something is **absorbed** when it is sucked up or taken in by something else.
Cognate (Spanish) **absorbido**

atmosphere (at' mə sfir) *n.* The **atmosphere** holds all the air around Earth's surface.
Cognate (Spanish) **atmósfera**

equator (i kwa' tər) *n.* The **equator** is an invisible circle that divides Earth into two equal parts.

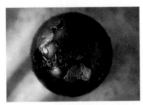

global warming (glō' bəl wor' ming) *n.* **Global warming** happens when gases created by human activity cause Earth's temperature to rise.

greenhouse gases (grēn' hows' gas' əs) *n.* Scientists call gases that trap heat near the Earth **greenhouse gases**.

surface (sər' fəs) *n.* The outside part of something is called its **surface**.

temperature (tem'pər chur) *n.* **Temperature** is a measure of how hot or cold something is.
Cognate (Spanish) **temperatura**

theory (thē ə re) *n.* A **theory** is a statement that may be true, but no one has proven it yet.
Cognate (Spanish) **teoría**

HEATING with SUNLIGHT

READ To Find Out — Why are some places on Earth warmer than others?

Do you have a light in your room? Have you ever put your hand near the light bulb? When your hand gets closer to the light, your hand gets hotter. Your other hand is not close to the light, so it is cool. In the same way, certain places on Earth are warmer when others are cool. Why does that happen?

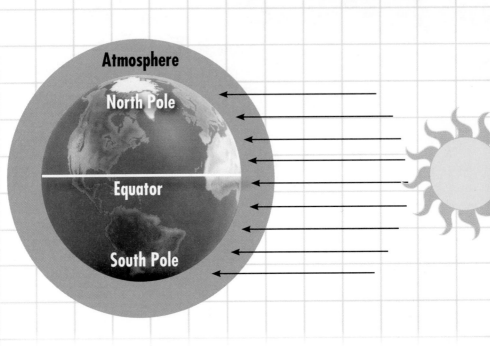

Light and Heat

The light from the Sun warms Earth's **surface**. To see why some parts of Earth are warmer than others, imagine you have a ball and a flashlight. Earth is the ball and the Sun is the flashlight. When you shine the light on the ball, it is bright in the middle, and darker at the top and bottom. The Sun shines on Earth the same way. The warmest area on Earth is at the **equator**. The equator gets the most sunlight, so it also gets the most heat.

Where are the coldest places on Earth? Darker areas get less light and are colder. The **North Pole** and the **South Pole** are the coldest place on Earth.

LET'S TALK! Why are the North Pole and South Pole cold?

---

surface the outside of something
equator imaginary line around the middle of Earth
North Pole the place farthest north on Earth
South Pole the place farthest south on Earth

Why Doesn't Earth Get Too Hot?

Why doesn't Earth become hotter and hotter as it gets more heat from the Sun? The Earth cools itself. The heat from the Sun is **absorbed** by land, trees, pavement, soil, and oceans. Then the heat leaves Earth and goes back into space.

But some gases around Earth **trap** some of the heat. These gases are called **greenhouse gases**. Think about how a greenhouse stays warm inside. A greenhouse has glass walls. The glass lets sunlight in, but it traps the heat inside the room. The greenhouse gases in Earth's **atmosphere** also trap heat too.

Greenhouse Effect

Sun

Earth

---

absorbed taken in by
trap to keep in
greenhouse gases gases that trap heat
atmosphere gases around the Earth

83

Is Earth Getting Warmer?

People around the world are using more oil, gas, and **coal**. This causes more and more greenhouse gases to go into the atmosphere. These gases keep the heat in. Some people worry that the greenhouse gases cause the **temperature** of Earth to get warmer each year. This **theory** is called **global warming**. Many scientists say that global warming can cause Earth to become warmer. If this theory is true, maybe one day even the North Pole will become warm!

coal hard black substance found in the Earth and burned for fuel
temperature measure of heat
theory idea
global warming Earth getting hotter

What Do You Think? Talk with a partner about greenhouse gases. Then draw a diagram showing how greenhouse gases trap heat on Earth's surface. Compare your diagram with you partner's diagram. Where is the warm air trapped on your diagram?

The Changes Around Us

Talk About It!

What is your favorite type of weather?

READ • Climate

Prepare To Read

Literary Element Text Features

Text features are ways of showing information. Some text features are:

- ❱ titles   ❱ heads and subheads
- ❱ lists   ❱ photos
- ❱ maps, graphs, and charts

Text features help you quickly understand what you are reading.

Practice Read the text in the box. What text features does it have?

Did You Know?
- ❱ The Great Pyramids are in Egypt.
- ❱ The pyramids were giant tombs for the kings of Egypt.

The Great Pyramids

Reading Skill Analyze Text Structure

Authors use **text structure** to organize ideas in the text. One type of text structure is time order. This text structure helps you understand the order of events. When you analyze text structure, you think about why the text is organized the way it is.

As you read, complete the graphic organizer in the *Expressions Practice Book*.

Climate
I. What Is Climate?
A. What Causes Different Climates?   1.   2.
B. Local Effects on Climate   1.   2.

Vocabulary for Climate

Read the words and definitions below.

climate (klī′ mət) *n.* **Climate** is the average weather found in a place.
Cognate (Spanish) **clima**

glaciers (glā′ shərz) *n.* Large sheets of ice that move slowly over land are **glaciers**.
Cognate (Spanish) **glaciares**

humidity (hyū mi′ də tē) *n.* The amount of water in the air is **humidity**. Cognate (Spanish) **humedad**

meteorite (mē′ tē ə rīt) *n.* A **meteorite** is a large rock from space. Cognate (Spanish) **meteorito**

precipitation (pri si pə tā′ shən) *n.* Water that falls to Earth as rain, snow, and hail is **precipitation**.
Cognate (Spanish) **precipitación**

predict (pri dikt′) *v.* When you guess what will happen in the future, you **predict**.
Cognate (Spanish) **predecir**

regions (rē′ jəns) *n.* **Regions** are areas that have common characteristics.
Cognate (Spanish) **regiones**

volcano (väl kā′ nō) *n.* A hill or mountain over an opening in the earth where lava and gasses come out is a **volcano**. Cognate (Spanish) **volcán**

Climate

READD
To Find Out

Why are there different climates?

Do you think it is cold in the month of February? February is snowy and freezing for most people in the United States. But February is the warmest month of the year for someone living in Brazil. Weather is different all over the world. While some **regions** are dry and hot, other places are always rainy. Some places are even covered with ice!

How do we know what kind of weather each region has? Scientists measure temperature, **humidity**, sunny days, and **precipitation** to find the average weather in a region. The measurements show the type of weather that happens most of the time. This is the **climate** of a region.

---

regions areas
humidity water in the air
precipitation rainfall or snowfall
climate average weather

What Causes Different Climates?

Did you ever go to the beach on a hot day? It feels cooler near the water and hotter just a few steps away. Climate can change that quickly.

It is cooler near the ocean and hotter in a **desert**. Do you wonder why? Wind is part of the reason. Winds that travel across ocean water can be warm or cool. These winds blow over the **coasts** along the ocean. The winds heat or cool land along the coast. This makes the coast warmer or cooler than the land farther from the water.

desert dry, often sandy area
coasts the land next to an ocean

What if you are in the city? Buildings, streets, sidewalks, and parking lots make the air around them warmer. That is why cities often feel warmer than areas with many trees or open land.

Regions with mountains have their own type of climate. When air goes up one side of a mountain, it loses its **moisture**. The moisture falls as rain or snow. That side of a mountain is cool and wet. The air becomes dry near the top of a mountain. Air going down makes the other side of the mountain dry and warm.

LET'S TALK! Describe the climate in different regions.

---

moisture small drops of water

READ To Find Out ▷ How has climate changed over time?

The Big Freeze

Long ago, the sun didn't warm the Earth as it does now. The Earth became very cold. Why did this climate change happen? Some scientists think that smoke and dust blocked the sunlight. Did a **meteorite crash** into Earth and create the dust? Did a **volcano erupt**? Scientists aren't sure what caused the climate to become so cold.

freeze to become ice
meteorite rock from space
crash to hit hard
volcano hole in Earth that releases lava
erupt blow up

A World of Ice

About 20,000 years ago, the climate of North America was very different than it is today. It was very cold. Large sheets of ice and snow called **glaciers** formed. These glaciers slowly covered most of North America. Then, the climate changed, and most of the glaciers **melted**. Scientists are not sure why the climate changed.

> **LET'S TALK!** What events can change climate?

---

glaciers large sheets of ice
melted changed from a solid to a liquid due to heat

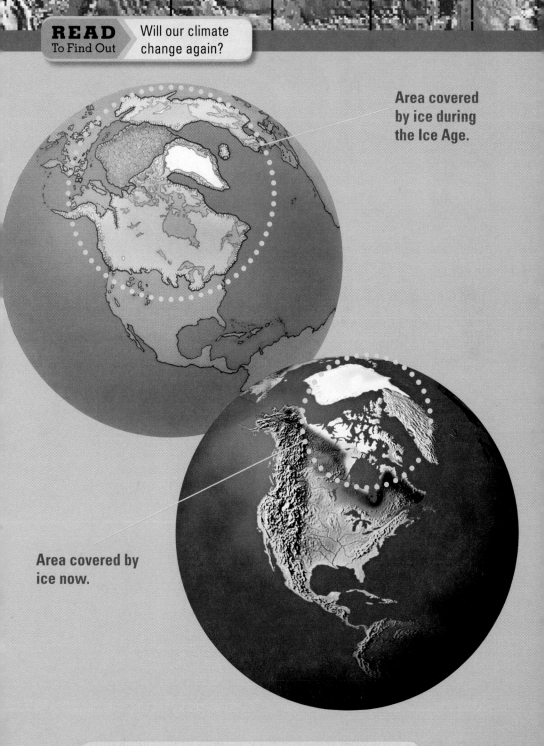

Will our climate
change again?

Area covered
by ice during
the Ice Age.

Area covered by
ice now.

Once, ice covered much of North America.
Would ice have covered where you live today?

93

The Next Change

Scientists continue to study how climate changes. They want to know what will happen if the temperature of Earth rises. How do they try to **predict** the next change?

Scientists study the ice that covers the North Pole and South Pole. They measure how quickly these ice caps and glaciers are melting. If the ice melts quickly, the water levels in the oceans may rise. People living near the coast will have **flooding**. Some scientists predict **storms** will get stronger if the climate warms around the world. They predict more land may become deserts.

The weather around the world has always changed. Nobody is really sure how our climate will change in the future. So keep watching the weather reports!

---

predict to guess what will happen
flooding an overflowing of water onto land that is usually dry
storms weather such as rain, snow, wind, thunder, or lightning

What Do You Think? Look back at the maps of North America on page 93. With a partner, compare the climate in your region to the climate when the Earth was very cold.

Life Lessons

Talk About It!

How do you feel when someone tricks you?

READ ▸ • The Monkey and the Crocodile

Prepare To Read

Character

A **character** is a person or an animal in a story. Sometimes folktales have a character called a **trickster**.

❯ Tricksters are smarter than bigger and stronger characters in the story.

❯ Tricksters may also be brave, sneaky, quick, or funny.

Practice Read the paragraph. Then answer the questions with a partner.

Crow loved to eat fish. Crow could not catch a fish by himself. Bear was very good at catching fish. In fact, Bear had just pulled a fish from the river with his paw. Crow wanted that fish. He hopped over to a pile of dirt and pretended to eat it. "This is so tasty!" cried Crow. Bear came over to see if he could steal this tasty food from Crow. When he did, Crow hopped over to the fish. He grabbed the fish and flew away.

1. Who is the trickster in this story?
2. How does Crow compare to Bear?
3. How does Crow trick Bear?
4. What does Bear learn in this story?

As you read, complete the graphic organizer in the *Expressions Practice Book*.

Character	Words that describe personality	Words that describe appearance	Is the character a trickster?
Monkey			
Crocodile			
Frogs			

Vocabulary for The Monkey and the Crocodile

Read the words and definitions below.

amazed (ə māzd') *v.* When you are **amazed**, you find something very surprising.

bank (bangk') *n.* A **bank** is a strip of land along the edge of a river.

cleverness (kle' ver nes) *n.* **Cleverness** helps a person think quickly to solve a problem.

crowd (krowd') *n.* A **crowd** is a large group of people or animals standing together.

excited (ik sī' təd) *v.* You are **excited** when you feel happy about doing something.

message (me' sij) *n.* Information sent from one person to another is a **message**.

Cognate (Spanish) **mensaje**

shivered (shiv' ərd) *v.* Someone has **shivered** when they have shaken from being cold.

snarled (snärld') *v.* When an animal has **snarled**, it has growled and shown its teeth.

The Monkey and the Crocodile

READ To Find Out — Why does Monkey like to swing in the trees?

Monkey loved to swing from tree to tree in the forest. He moved as fast as Cheetah, the fastest cat that ever ran. Monkey lived up high in the treetops, where he slept, ate, and played.

Monkey liked it when the other animals watched him swing. He swung faster when they were looking at him. The other animals were **amazed** and happy to watch Monkey. He often made them laugh.

The animals watched Monkey for another reason, too. Monkey was a messy eater. He usually dropped bits of fruit from the tree. The **crowd** ate the fruit Monkey dropped.

One day the animals came to watch Monkey's show. Every animal was **excited** to see the show except for Crocodile.

---

amazed surprised
crowd group
excited looking forward to

"Every day I watch Monkey fly around in the treetops," Crocodile **grumbled**. "I am tired of sliding on my belly along the ground. I always visit my friend Monkey. It's time for Monkey to come visit me in the river!" Crocodile lifted his large head and swung his long nose from side to side.

"Hey! Frogs! Listen to me!" Crocodile yelled. The frightened frogs hopped over to the angry Crocodile.

"I have a job for you! Tell Monkey it's time he visited me!" Crocodile said. The frogs **shivered** with fear as Crocodile opened his **jaws** wide and snapped them shut. Crocodile snapped his jaws until the frogs hopped away to give Monkey the **message**.

Monkey laughed when he heard the message. "My friend Crocodile knows I do not swim," Monkey said to the frogs, "and I know Crocodile enjoys walking on the ground and lying on his belly. Go back to my friend Crocodile and tell him I won't visit his river. He must visit me here."

---

grumbled complained
shivered shook
jaws set of teeth
message thought to be shared

LET'S TALK! Why does Monkey laugh when he hears Crocodile's message?

READ
To Find Out

How will the frogs get Monkey to visit Crocodile?

The frogs returned to the river. Crocodile got angry when he heard Monkey's **reply.** "I will make him sorry he said those words!" Crocodile **roared.** "In fact, I think I'll eat him!" Crocodile said. He snapped his jaws even louder than before.

reply answer
roared said deepy and loudly

101

"Go back to Monkey and bring him to me," said Crocodile to the frogs, "If you don't go, I will eat you for my next meal!"

The frogs went back to Monkey. "Please, Monkey," **begged** the frogs, "you must come back with us to visit Crocodile. If you don't, he will eat us!"

"But I do not swim," Monkey told the frogs. "I cannot visit Crocodile at his home in the river."

"You don't have to get into the water," said the frogs. "Crocodile will crawl out onto the **bank**. You can stand on the bank and talk to him. Crocodile just wants to show you his nice home."

The frogs begged Monkey until he agreed to visit the river. But monkey did not walk to the river. He swung from **branches** until he reached Crocodile's home.

---

begged asked as a favor
bank strip of land by a river
branches part of a tree that grows out of the trunk

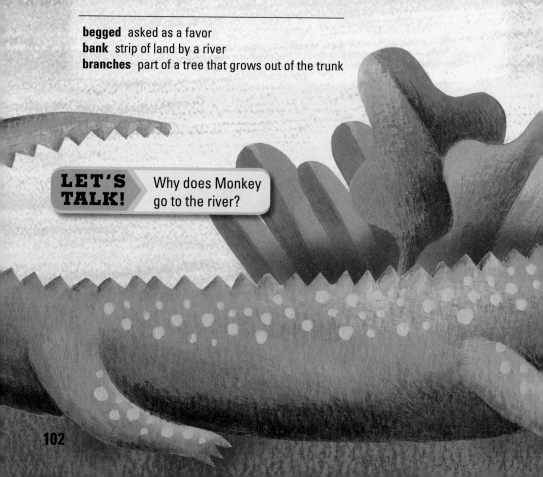

LET'S TALK! Why does Monkey go to the river?

Crocodile watched the trees until he saw Monkey come down and walk along the riverbank. Crocodile crawled out of the water, smiling and licking his lips. He thought Monkey would make a good meal. Crocodile **snarled** at Monkey and trapped him against a tree.

"I have you trapped, Monkey," Crocodile said. "First, I am going to eat your heart."

Monkey had always thought it would be hard to be Crocodile's friend. Now he was sure of it. Monkey decided to use his **cleverness** to get away.

"Crocodile, my friend," Monkey said, "You should have told me you wanted to eat my heart. I'm sorry, but I left my heart in the tree where I live."

"What?" Crocodile roared angrily.

"I can get my heart for you," Monkey **offered**. "It will only take a minute. Then you can have it to eat."

---

snarled growled and shown teeth
cleverness tricks for solving problems
offered shared the idea

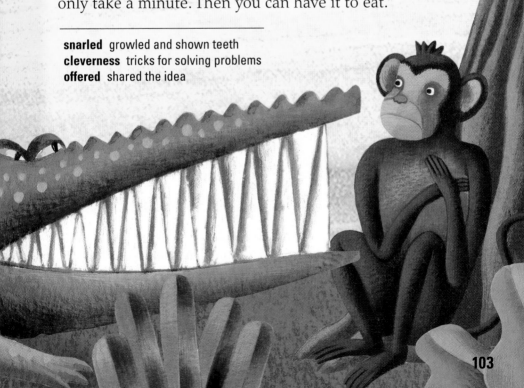

103

"Yes, hurry!" Crocodile said. He **grinned** and watched Monkey hurry back up the tree. Monkey climbed to a high branch. "Ha, ha, ha!" Monkey laughed, "I can't believe you thought my heart was in the tree! You are silly, Crocodile. My heart is inside of me. Now I am safe in the tree!"

Monkey knew he was lucky to get away this time. Next time, he would be more **cautious** when he chose a friend.

Crocodile slipped back into the cold river. He was angry that Monkey got away. He was also sad. Now he had lost his only friend!

---

grinned smiled
cautious careful

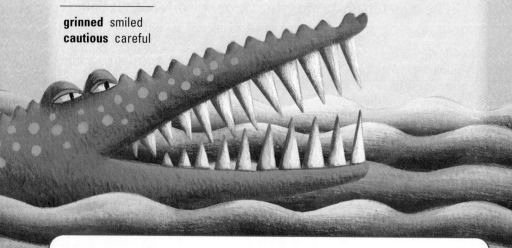

What Do You Think? What lesson can you learn from this story? Discuss your answers in a small group. Use the sentence frame below to help you get started.

I think that the lesson of this story is ___ because ___.

A Tricky Tale

Talk About It!

When is it important to be clever?

READ
- Clever Jackal Gets Away
- Brer Rabbit Earns a Dollar-a-Minute

Reading Skill Compare and Contrast Characters

A **character** can be a person, animal, or other living thing. Characters have traits, or ways they look, act, and feel. For example, a trickster is a character that may look or act silly but is very smart. Tricksters make other characters look foolish.

When you **compare and contrast characters**, you look for similarities and differences.

Comparing and contrasting characters will help you understand a story better.

As you read, ask yourself the following questions:

> ❯ How are the main characters the same?
> ❯ How are the main characters different?

As you read, complete the graphic organizer in the *Expressions Practice Book*.

Character	Words that describe personality	Words that describe appearance	Is the character a trickster?
The Lion			
Brer Bear			
Brer Rabbit			
Toad			
Donkey			

Vocabulary for Clever Jackal Gets Away

Read the words and definitions below.

admired (əd mī ərd') *v.* If you **admired** someone, you felt that he or she was special.
Cognate (Spanish) **admirar**

shrugged (shrəg' d) *v.* If a person **shrugged**, his or her shoulders quickly moved up and down.

crushed (krəsht') *v.* When a thing is **crushed**, it is pressed flat by something heavy.

sniffing (snif' fing) *v.* When someone is **sniffing**, they are breathing through their nose to smell the air.

escape (is kāp') *v.* When you **escape**, you get away from someone who is trying to catch you.
Cognate (Spanish) **escapar**

strength (strength') *n.* A person who can lift heavy things has a lot of **strength**.

instantly (in' stənt lē) *adv.* Something happens **instantly** when it happens right away.
Cognate (Spanish) **instantáneamente**

tale (tāl') *n.* A **tale** is a story that many people know.

Clever Jackel Gets Away

READ To Find Out — Why is Sipho sometimes called "Jackal?"

"Come here, my child," Gogo said to her grandchild Sipho one evening. "Sipho, cleverness is very important. It has helped the rabbit get out of the cooking pot more than once!"

Little Sipho replied, "The jackal is also a **clever** animal, isn't he, Gogo?"

When Sipho was a baby, Gogo gave him the nickname Jackal. Sipho was proud of his nickname. Sipho **admired** jackals because they moved so quickly. He **imagined** he was as fast as a jackal.

Gogo laughed and looked at Sipho, "Yes, my boy. You are right! Jackal is a very clever animal. But sometimes he is too clever for his own good," Gogo said.

---

clever intelligent
admired wanted to be like
imagined had a picture in mind

108

"Please, Gogo, tell me a **tale** about Jackal!" Sipho begged.

"All right, my child. Listen and learn," Gogo said. And she told this story.

One day long ago, Jackal was walking along a rocky path. As always, he had his nose to the ground, **sniffing** for something to eat. He hoped that he might catch a lizard or two.

Suddenly, Jackal saw something move ahead of him. Lion was coming toward him!"

"Oh, no!" Jackal thought.

tale a story
sniffing using his nose to smell

109

Jackal knew he could not **escape**. Jackal had played him for a fool many times. Jackal was sure Lion wanted to take revenge on him. But Jackal's clever mind worked quickly. **Instantly**, he had a plan.

Big rocks hung above Jackal. He quickly hid below them. Then he yelled loudly for help.

"Help, help!" Jackal yelled as loudly as he could. Lion was so surprised that he stopped in his tracks.

LET'S TALK! Why is Jackal afraid of Lion?

escape get away from
instantly right away

"Oh, great King Lion! Help! Those big rocks above us are about to fall! We will both be **crushed**! Oh, great Lion, save us!" Jackal bent down and covered his head with his paws. Lion believed Jackal was very afraid!

Lion looked at the rocks and became very afraid too. He thought the rocks might fall on them.

"Hurry, Lion," Jackal begged. "Use your great **strength** to hold up the rocks!

Lion put his big shoulder against the rocks and pushed.

"Oh, thank you, great King Lion!" said Jackal.

---

crushed   pushed down and hurt
strength   power

"You hold the rocks up. I will get that log over there. Then the log will hold up the rocks and we will both be **saved**!" Jackal promised.

As Lion pushed on the rocks, Jackal ran out of sight. Now Lion was alone. He used all his strength to push the rocks up, but the rocks would not move!

"How long did Lion stay there?" Sipho asked Gogo.

Gogo **shrugged**. "Who knows? Lion pushed until he **realized** that Jackal had tricked him again. That clever Jackal escaped!" she said.

"Yes, Gogo! Cleverness is very important!" said Sipho with a smile.

---

saved made safe from harm
shrugged moved the shoulders as if to say, "I don't know."
realized came to understand

What Do You Think? Jackal tells Lion that the rocks will fall. Why does Lion believe Jackal? Talk with a partner. Use the sentence frame below.

I think Lion believes Jackal because___.

Vocabulary for Vocabulary for Brer Rabbit
Earns a Dollar-a-Minute Read the words and definitions below.

earning (ər' ning) *v.* When you do work to get money, you are **earning** it.

explanation (ek splə nā' shən) *n.* An **explanation** tells how or why something happens.
Cognate (Spanish) **explicación**

ripen (rī pən') *v.* As fruits or vegetables grow ready to eat, they **ripen**.

sneaked (snēkt') *v.* If you **sneaked** somewhere, you moved there secretly.

suspected (sə spek' təd) *v.* When you have **suspected** another person, you thought that person did something wrong.
Cognate (Spanish) **sospechar**

thief (thēf') *n.* A **thief** is someone who steals something.

threatened (thre' tənd) *v.* Someone has **threatened** when they have said they will harm someone else.

trespasser (tres' pəs ər) *n.* A **trespasser** goes in places where people must not enter.

Brer Rabbit
Earns a Dollar-A-Minute

READ To Find Out — What does Brer Rabbit do to Brer Fox's peanuts?

Brer Fox worked hard to plant his peanuts. Soon, the peanuts began to **ripen**.

Brer Rabbit saw the tasty peanuts. He **sneaked** in and took most of them. When Brer Fox came back to his garden, there were hardly any peanuts left!

The hard-working fox was very upset. Who was stealing his peanuts? He **suspected** Brer Rabbit. Brer Fox made a trap that would catch the **trespasser**.

The next morning, Brer Rabbit slipped through the hole in the fence. Suddenly Brer Rabbit was hanging upside down! He knew he got caught.

Brer Rabbit was thinking of an **explanation** when he heard someone coming. It was Brer Bear. Brer Rabbit had an idea.

---

ripen to become fully grown and ready to eat
sneaked secretly
suspected thought that he had done something wrong
trespasser someone who goes somewhere they should not
explanation what to say

"Hello, Brer Bear," he called.

"Hello, Brer Rabbit," Brer Bear said. "How are you? Why are you up in the tree?"

"I'm **earning** a dollar-a-minute from Brer Fox."

"What for?" Brer Bear asked.

"That fox will pay anyone a dollar-a-minute to keep the crows away," said the rabbit.

The rabbit asked Brer Bear if he would like the job. The bear thought it was a good idea. So Brer Bear took Brer Rabbit down. Soon the bear was in his place and he was hanging upside down!

"I've caught the peanut **thief**," Brer Fox cried when he saw Brer Bear. Brer Fox yelled and **threatened** to hit Brer Bear with his walking stick. Poor Brer Bear got down and ran away.

---

earning being paid
thief one who steals
threatened promised to harm

Brer Rabbit knew that Brer Bear would be very angry at him. The rabbit hid in the mud beside a pond. He tried to make his eyes stick out, just like a bullfrog. Soon Brer Bear came down the road looking for the rabbit.

"Hello, Brer Bullfrog," Brer Bear said when he saw Brer Rabbit's eyes sticking out. "Have you seen Brer Rabbit?"

Brer Rabbit croaked like a frog. "Brer Rabbit ran down the road," he said.

"Thank you," said the bear. He went down the road.

The clever rabbit was safe. His tricks had worked again. Brer Rabbit jumped out of the mud and ran home.

"I'm hungry," he said. "Now, how can I get Brer Fox's peanuts again?"

What Do You Think? What lessons do you think the fox, the bear, and the rabbit can teach you? Talk about it with a partner. Use the sentence frame below.

I think the ___ can teach me that ___.

Writing Workshop

Writing a Functional Document

Writing That Gives Direction
A **functional document** shares facts, instructions, and other types of information. People may use functional documents to learn information about a process, an event, or a service.

Writing Assignment
For this Writing Workshop, you will write an **invitation** for others to join you on a trip to a place of interest. Your invitation will include a map and directions. Write your invitation for your classmates and your teacher. They will be your audience.

WRITING PLAN

> Make the purpose of the document clear.

> Present information in a clear order that makes sense.

> Include supporting details to create interest and inform the reader.

> Use visual clues and text features to set off important information.

Writing Model

COME SEE THE WORLD OF THE PAST!

Who: Alan, Carlos, Juma, Brianna, and Marie

What: a trip to Sequoia National Park

Where: 140 miles from Merced, CA

When: Saturday, April 19

Why: hike and outdoor picnic

How: Alan's dad will drive

How to Get There
1. Take HWY 99 southeast to Fresno.
2. Then take HWY 180 east to Sequoia National Park.

Prewrite

1. **Gather Ideas**
   Make a list of places you would like to visit with friends. Write down anything you know about each place. Research one or two places that look the most interesting. Find travel directions for your trip. Take notes about what you might do on your visit.

2. **Choose a Place**
   Read the notes from your research. Then choose the place you would most like to visit. Use this sentence frame to explain your choice:

   I want to visit ___ because ___.

3. **Get Organized**
   Use your notes to make two charts. One chart will list invitation details. One chart will list trip details to help you make a map and directions.

Invitation Details (5Ws and H)	
Who:	the people being invited
What:	a trip to place of interest
Where:	the location of the place
When:	the dates of the trip
Why:	the reason for the trip
How:	a way that people can get there

Directions and Map	
Starting Point:	Merced, CA
Ending Point:	Sequoia National Park, CA
Distance:	140 miles
How to Get There:	Take Highway 99 southeast to Fresno. Then take Highway 180 to the park.

Draft

1. **Start Writing**
   Use your notes and your charts to write your invitation.

2. **Add to Your Draft**
   Think about your **purpose** for writing the invitation and your **audience**. Your first sentence should make your readers want to go with you on your trip.

> Come with me and see the world as it was thousands of years ago!

Use good **organization**. List the most important details first in the invitation. Give directions from start to finish. Place details correctly on the map.

> Who: Alan, Carlos, Juma, Brianna, and Marie

> When: Saturday, April 19

USE GOOD WRITING TRAITS: CONVENTIONS

Conventions are the rules of language. Follow rules for grammar, usage, spelling, capitalization, and punctuation. Your writing will be easier for readers to understand.

Read the example below. Notice that it is not a complete sentence. It uses a colon to label an important detail. This is a punctuation convention.

> Why: to hike and have an outdoor picnic

Check your draft to be sure you have followed the rules of language. Ask yourself: Did I use conventions to make my ideas easy to understand?

Revise

Now it's time to revise your draft. This step helps you make your writing better so others will want to read it.

1. **Read Your Invitation** Ask yourself these questions:
   - Are all the important details correct?
   - Did you forget any important information?
   - Does the invitation list the most important details first?

2. **Show Your Invitation** Trade drafts with a partner. Answer these questions as you read your partner's document:
   - Are the purpose and audience clear?
   - Do the directions make sense?
   - Are the map features easy to understand?
   - Do supporting details add interest and make information more clear?

3. **Make Your Changes** Talk with your partner to help you decide what changes you need to make. Then revise your invitation.

> **Technology** Use the design features of your word processing software to add or create graphics that will make your invitation more exciting. You can use graphic software to create a map, or you can search for a map on the Internet to include with your invitation.

Edit and Proofread

1. **Proofread Your Invitation** Reread your invitation one sentence at a time. Look for mistakes in capitalization, punctuation, or spelling. Use the proofreading symbols in the chart on page 353 to mark changes.

2. **Check Your Information** Are all your important details easy to read and understand? Is all your information true? Make changes if you need to.

Grammar Focus: Capitalization

Capitalize all proper nouns in your writing. Proper nouns name specific people, places, things, and ideas. Look at the examples to see how to fix problems.

The Problem: A proper noun is not capitalized.

> Where: 140 miles from merced, CA

The Solution: Capitalize the name of a specific place.

> Where: 140 miles from Merced, CA

The Problem: General direction words are capitalized.

> Sequoia National Park is 140 miles Southeast of Merced.

The Solution: Use lowercase letters for words that describe general directions.

> Sequoia National Park is 140 miles southeast of Merced.

3. **Make a Final Copy** Make the corrections that you marked. If you are working on the computer, print out the corrected work. If not, rewrite it.

Present

Here are some ways to share your writing.

- Give your invitation to friends to read and ask them for their comments.
- Imagine you work at the place you wrote about in your invitation. Have a partner interview you about why this place is interesting.

⬛ Speaking, Listening, and Viewing Workshop

Informative Presentation

Activity

1. **Connect to Your Writing**
   Give an informative oral presentation to your classmates. Use the invitation and map you made for the Writing Workshop on pages 117–121.

2. **Plan Your Presentation**
   Reread your invitation and map. Mark the parts that you want to include in your presentation. Use these tips to help you prepare.
   - Include details for the 5 Ws and H of your trip.
   - Use facts that are clear and true.
   - Choose exciting words to describe your trip.
   - Create strong visuals that support your ideas and are easy to see.

3. **Practice Your Presentation**
   Practice your presentation in front of a mirror. Watch your facial expressions and gestures. Listen to the volume and style of your voice. Practice until you feel ready to give your presentation.

4. **Give Your Presentation**
   - Speak clearly.
   - Be sure everyone can see your visuals.
   - Speak slowly when giving details that might be confusing.

Listening to Learn
As you listen to another student's presentation, take notes. Use the sentence frames below to learn more about what you hear.
- I could not understand one part. Please review ___.
- I was interested in ___. Please tell me more.

Not Like All The Rest

Talk About It!

What can you learn from pets?

READ • "Roger the Dog"

Prepare To Read

Alliteration and Assonance

Alliteration is when consonant sounds are repeated at the beginning of words. For example, notice how the *h* sound repeats in this sentence: *Hal had on a heavy hat.*

Assonance is when the same vowel sound is repeated in a line of poetry. Listen for the long *e* sound as you read this sentence: *Eat the sweet fruit from the tree!*

❯ To figure out **alliteration**, look for the same letter at the beginning of words.

❯ To figure out **assonance**, listen for a vowel sound that repeats.

Practice Read the sentences. Which one has alliteration? Which one has assonance? Explain your answer.

> 1. My dog wheezes as she sleeps.
>
> 2. My dog Rover races and romps in the rain.

As you read, complete the graphic organizer in the *Expressions Practice Book*.

Title of Poem: Roger the Dog

Alliteration: Initial Consonant Sounds	Number of Times Repeated	Assonance: Vowel Sounds	Number of Times Repeated

Vocabulary for "Roger the Dog"

Read the words and definitions below.

bakes (bāks') *v.* When food cooks in an oven, it **bakes**.

lug (ləg') *v.* You **lug** something that is heavy or hard to carry.

miner (mī' nər) *n.* A **miner** digs into the ground for items such as gold or coal.

(Spanish) **minero / minera**

roll (rōl') *v.* You **roll** something when you turn it over many times.

romp (romp') *v.* When animals or people **romp**, they move around in a playful way.

scratch (skrach') *v.* When something bothers your skin, you **scratch** it.

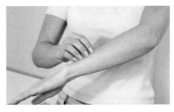

snoring (snor' əng) *adj.* The rough breathing sound people make when they sleep is a **snoring** sound.

wheezes (wēz' əz) *v.* When someone **wheezes**, the person breathes in a noisy way.

Roger the Dog

by Ted Hughes

READ To Find Out   What does Roger like to do?

Asleep he **wheezes** at his ease.

He only wakes to **scratch** his fleas.

He **hogs** the fire, he **bakes** his head

As if it were a loaf of bread.

---

wheezes breathes in a noisy way
scratch to rub his skin
hogs takes all the space in front of
bakes makes it very hot

He's just a sack of **snoring** dog,

You can **lug** him like a log.

You can **roll** him with your foot.

He'll stay snoring where he's put.

Take him out for exercise

He'll roll in **cowclap** up to his eyes.

---

snoring the loud breathing sound when someone is asleep
lug to drag something that is heavy
roll to turn over
cowclap dirt from animals

He will not race, he will not **romp**.

He saves his strength for **gobble and chomp**.

He'll work as hard as you could wish

Emptying the dinner dish,

Then he **flops** flat, and digs down deep,

Like a **miner**, into sleep.

---

romp play and jump
gobble and chomp eating
flops falls down
miner a worker who digs into the ground

What Do You Think? Describe Roger to a partner. Then listen to how your partner describes the dog. Use the sentence frames below. Together, draw a picture of Roger.

Roger looks like ___.

The dog acts like ___.

Let's Look at China!

Talk About It!

What does food show about different cultures?

READ
- Chinese Food and Drink
- Chinese Family Life

Prepare To Read

Literary Element Description

Description is an explanation of a person, place, thing, or event. The description in a text helps readers see, hear, smell, taste, and touch what they read.

Practice Read the paragraph. Which details help you see, hear, smell, taste, and touch?

> Elena sat alone on the beach. She breathed in the salty air. She felt the sand burn her bare feet. Then she heard a wave crash on the shore. She felt small before the huge, blue ocean.

Reading Skill Analyze Cultural Context

People from different cultures have different customs, or ways of doing things. **Cultural context** is the customs and beliefs that a group of people share. When you **analyze cultural context**, you think about the characters' customs and beliefs. You also think about when and where the story takes place.

As you read, complete the graphic organizer in the *Expressions Practice Book*.

Detail	What It Reveals

Vocabulary for Chinese Food and Drink

Read the words and definitions below.

ancient (ān' shənt) *adj.* Something that is very old is **ancient**.

boil (boil') *v.* When you cook a liquid until it is very hot and bubbling, you **boil** it.

custom (kəs' təm) *n.* A cultural practice or tradition is a **custom**.
Cognate (Spanish) **costumbre**

expensive (ik spen' siv) *adj.* Something that costs more than usual is **expensive**.

population (pä' pyə lā' shən) *n.* All the people who live in a certain area are the **population**.

spices (spī' sez) *n.* **Spices** add flavor to food. Some spices are cinnamon, pepper, and ginger.

utensils (yu ten' səlz) *n.* When people use forks and knives to eat, they are using **utensils**.

variety (və rī' ə tē) *n.* When you have a **variety**, you have different kinds of one thing.

Chinese Food and Drink

READ To Find Out — What are some foods used in Chinese cooking?

Have you ever eaten lychee or longan fruit? Have you ever tasted ginger or anise? People have used these foods and **spices** in Chinese cooking for thousands of years.

lychee fruit

Main Grains

Rice is part of most Chinese meals. People have grown this grain in the warm, wet climate of southern China for more than 5,000 years. The people in **ancient** China cooked rice the same way they do today. They **boil** the rice in water or they steam it.

Millet is a grain that grows in northern China where the **climate** is dry and cool. Millet does not need much rain to grow, so it became a **main crop** in that part of China. People boil millet and eat it like hot cereal.

---

spices flavors that you add to food
ancient very old
boil cook in very hot water
climate the weather pattern in a certain place
main very important
crop plants grown on a farm

Fruits and Vegetables

People grew lychee and longan fruits in ancient China. Those fruits are still **popular** today. They also grew vegetables such as snow peas, cucumbers, and Chinese cabbage. These fruits and vegetables gave the rice a **variety** of flavors.

Tea Time

For thousands of years, tea has been an important part of Chinese culture. People make tea from the leaves of the tea plant. At first, people used tea leaves as a **medicine**. Later, people boiled tea leaves in water to make a drink. The Chinese make and serve tea in a certain way. This **custom** is the Chinese tea ceremony.

popular used often or a lot
variety different kinds
medicine something used to cure or heal
custom a tradition

Quick Sticks

Have you ever tried to eat with chopsticks? The Chinese people invented these **utensils** for a good reason. At one time, the **population** began to grow rapidly. The people cut down trees and planted crops. **Fewer** trees meant less wood for fire. People began to chop food into small pieces that could cook quickly.

People also needed a utensil to pick up the bite-size food. Chopsticks were the perfect tool. The Chinese word for chopsticks is *kuaizi*, which means "quick little fellows." Chopsticks move tasty Chinese food quickly into hungry mouths!

tofu

snow peas

Tofu

Meat was very **expensive** in ancient China. Many people could not afford to buy it. Instead of meat, they ate tofu, a soft food made from soybeans. Tofu gave them protein just as meat would.

---

utensils tools for eating
population amount of people in a place
fewer not as many
expensive something that costs very much

What Do You Think? What foods are important to you? Talk with a partner. Use the sentence frames below.

Foods that are important to me are_____.

They are important because_____.

Vocabulary for Chinese Family Life

Read the words and definitions below.

elders (el′ dərz) *n.* Older people are **elders**.

respect (ri spekt′) *n.* When you speak and act very nicely to someone, you show **respect**.

fields (fēldz′) *n.* **Fields** are large areas of land where farmers grow crops.

society (sə sī′ ə tē) *n.* People living together in a group form a **society**.
Cognate (Spanish) **sociedad**

gather (ga′ thər) *v.* When people **gather**, they come together in a group.

support (sə port′) *v.* When you help or assist another person, you **support** him or her.

obey (ō bā′) *v.* When you do what someone tells you to do, you **obey**.

traditional (trə dish′ nəl) *adj.* When you do something **traditional**, you do it the way people have always done it.

Chinese Family Life

Who are the **members** of your family? In Chinese **society**, a family includes more than parents and children. They have **extended families**. Grandparents, aunts, uncles, and cousins are all important people in an extended family. Chinese families today do some of the same things Chinese families did long ago.

Family Life

Long ago in China, many families were farmers. Much of the land was good for growing rice, so many families worked on rice farms. Everyone in the family helped. The older children worked in the **fields**. Even small children had jobs. An extended family working together could do more work and have more food, money, and other things.

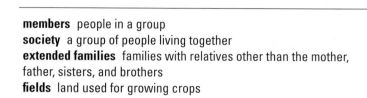

Beijing

Shangha

Xian

C H I N A

Guangzhou

TAIWAN

Hong Kong

members people in a group
society a group of people living together
extended families families with relatives other than the mother, father, sisters, and brothers
fields land used for growing crops

136

Learning the Rules

Imagine you are in an extended family. It would be large! With so many family members living together, how could you learn to get along with each other?

Chinese families taught that children must **respect** their **elders**, or those who are older. Younger children must **obey** older children. All children must obey their parents. Parents must obey the grandparents. In fact, the oldest person was the most important member of the family. This was how Chinese families **kept order**.

respect a way of nicely speaking and acting to someone
elders people who are older than you
obey do what someone says
kept order kept things under control and peaceful

Chinese Family Life Today

The extended family is still an important part of Chinese society. Family members may not live as close together as in the past, but they still **support** each other in many ways. Family members also **gather** to celebrate holidays and other events. Chinese New Year is one of the most important Chinese holidays. On this day, families **share traditional** foods, such as fish, noodles, and rice pudding. They use colorful decorations and dress in traditional clothes. Chinese families celebrate the holiday and remember the traditions of the past.

support to help another
gather come together
share to give some of what you have to others
traditional in the way that people have always done it

What Do You Think? Think about what life was like in ancient China. What do you think is different today? What might be the same? Talk about it with a partner.

Memories of Times Past

Talk About It!

Which memories are important to you?

READ
- "The Swing"
- "Thoughts"

Literary Element Rhyme

What is similar about the words *play* and *say*? They end with the same sound. These two words **rhyme**. In a poem, different words that end with the same sound create an **end rhyme**.

➤ The end rhyme of a poem can make a pattern. The pattern is the **rhyme scheme**.

➤ You can figure out the rhyme scheme by marking the lines that rhyme with letters.

This rhyme scheme is a, a, b, b:

Twinkle, twinkle, little star   a

How I wonder what you are. a

Up above the world so high b

Like a diamond in the sky.   b

Practice Read the two lists of words below. With a partner, figure out the rhyme scheme of each list.

1. clap	2. bright
trap	fall
sing	night
ring	wall

As you read, complete the graphic organizer in the *Expressions Practice Book*.

Poem Title: _____		
Line Number	**End Sound**	**Letter** (*a, b, c*)

Vocabulary for "The Swing"

Read the words and definitions below.

cattle (ka' təl) *n.* Cows and bulls that live on a farm or ranch are **cattle**.

swing (swing') *n.* A **swing** is a seat that moves back and forth.

countryside (kən' trē sīd') *n.* The **countryside** is open land where you see farms and animals.

wide (wīd') *adj.* Something that is a large distance from side to side is **wide**.

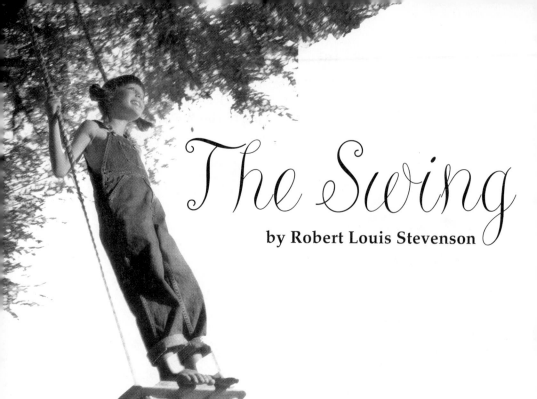

The Swing

by Robert Louis Stevenson

READ To Find Out — What is the setting of this poem?

How do you like to go up in a **swing**,
   Up in the air so blue?
"Oh, I do think it the **pleasantest** thing
   Ever a child can do!"

---

swing seat that moves back and forth
pleasantest the best; the most pleasant

"Up in the air and over the wall,

    Till I can see so **wide**,

Rivers and trees and **cattle** and all

    Over the **countryside**—

"Till I look down on the garden green

    Down on the **roof** so brown—

Up in the air I go flying again,

    Up in the air and down!"

---

wide far apart from side to side
cattle cows and bulls
countryside open land for farms and animals
roof the covering of a building

What Do You Think? What activity did you like to do when you were very young? Use the sentence frame below for your answer. Compare your answer with a partner's.

    When I was very young I liked to ___.

Vocabulary for "Thoughts"

Read the words and definitions below.

autumn (o' təm) *n.* **Autumn** is the period of time between summer and winter. It is one of the four seasons.

shore (shor') *n.* The area where land meets water is the **shore**.

flames (flāmz') *n.* When wood is on fire, it creates yellow and red **flames**.

tangy (tang'ē) *adj.* Something that has a strong taste is **tangy**.

Thoughts

READ
To Find Out

What does the speaker think about when it is autumn?

The tree-lined street is lit in gold
and red and orange, like **flames**,
the **autumn** air, so cool and **tangy**,
rings with children's games.

A windy whoosh of fallen leaves
comes swirling through the door–
why does it bring us memories
of summers at the **shore**?

Of chasing **breakers** in the surf
and running through the sand
with burning soles and curling toes,
and leaping down the strand

---

flames burning fire
autumn the season between summer and winter
tangy strong-flavored
shore where land meets the water
breakers large waves

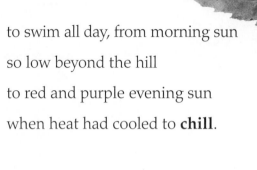

to swim all day, from morning sun

so low beyond the hill

to red and purple evening sun

when heat had cooled to **chill**.

So in this golden autumn time

we turn ourselves around

and let those thoughts, like **scattered** leaves,

fall slowly to the ground.

No beach, no sand, no sound of surf,

just sunset on the town,

filtered through the colored leaves

that **flutter** gently down.

---

chill cold
scattered in many places, far away from
each other
filtered passed through something
flutter move quickly, in a wavy motion

What Do You Think? What is your favorite time of the
year? Use the sentence frame below for your answer. Share
your ideas with a partner.

My favorite time of the year is ___ because___.

On My Way Forward

Talk About It!

How can learning to be patient help you grow?

READ ▸ "Will There Really Be a Morning?"

Literary Element   Rhythm and Meter

The **rhythm** of a poem is the pattern of beats. You can make rhythm by stressing some words more than others. When you stress a sound, you say it louder and with more force. **Meter** is a rhythm that is repeated over and over again. Music also has a rhythm and meter.

Practice Read the poem out loud. When you read an underlined word or word part, change your voice to stress it. Listen for a pattern as you read out loud.

> I'll <u>tell</u> you the <u>story</u> of <u>Jimmy Jet</u> —
> And you <u>know</u> what I <u>tell</u> you is <u>true</u>.
> He <u>loved</u> to watch his <u>TV set</u>
> <u>Almost</u> as <u>much</u> as <u>you</u>.

As you read, complete the graphic organizer in the *Expressions Practice Book*.

"Will There Really Be a Morning?"	
Verse Number	**Stressed Words and Syllables**

Read the words and definitions below.

famous (fa' məs) *adj.* Something that is very popular and well known is **famous**.

pilgrim (pil' grəm) *n.* A **pilgrim** is someone who travels a long way to find answers.

feathers (fe' thərs) *n.* Birds have **feathers** covering their bodies. They use them to fly.

sailor (sa' lər) *n.* A **sailor** is a person who works on a boat.

mountains (maun' tənz) *n.* **Mountains** are very large hills or land formations.

scholar (skä' lər) *n.* A **scholar** is someone who studies hard and knows a lot about one or more subjects.

Will There Really Be a Morning?

by Emily Dickinson

READ To Find Out — What is the speaker waiting for?

Will there really be a morning?

Is there such a thing as day?

Could I see it from the mountains

If I were as tall as they?

---

mountains large hills or land formations

Has it feet like water-lilies?
Has it **feathers** like a bird?
Is it brought from **famous** countries
Of which I have never heard?

---

feathers what covers a bird's body
famous popular; well known

Oh, some **scholar**! Oh, some **sailor**!

Oh, some **wise** man from the skies!

Please to tell a little **pilgrim**

Where the place called morning lies!

---

scholar well-educated person
sailor a person who works on a boat
wise smart; having good judgment
pilgrim someone who travels a long way to find answers

What Do You Think?   What would you tell this speaker if he or she came to you and asked these questions? Use the sentence frame and share your ideas with a partner.

The questions I would answer are ___ and ___.

My answers would be ___ and ___.

Learning Lessons

Talk About It!

What lessons can you learn from a story?

READ • Arachne

Prepare To Read

Literary Element Myth

Myths are traditional stories. Some myths are about gods and goddesses. Other myths are about heroes and monsters.

> Some myths explain something about nature.
> Many myths explain the customs and beliefs of a group of people.

As you read, ask yourself, what does this myth teach you about the world and other groups of people?

Practice Read the paragraph. What tells you that it is a myth?

> Hercules was strong and brave. He was the son of a god and a human woman. Hercules did many heroic things in his life. When he died, he became a god.

Reading Strategy Make Generalizations About Plot

Plot is what happens in a story. When you **make generalizations about plot**, you think about how the plot is like plots in other stories.

Think about

> what happens in the story.
> what lessons you learn from the myth.
> other myths you have read that are similar.

As you read, complete in the graphic organizer in the *Expressions Practice Book*.

Plot Elements

Similar Plot Elements in Another Myth

Generalizations About Myths

Vocabulary for Arachne

Read the words and definitions below.

challenge (cha'lənj) *n.* A **challenge** is an offer to face others in a game or contest.

insult (in'səlt) *n.* A rude or disrespectful action or speech is an **insult**.
Cognate (Spanish) **insulto**

contest (kän'test) *n.* A game or a race to see who can win is a **contest**.

loom (lüm') *n.* A machine for making fabric is a **loom**.

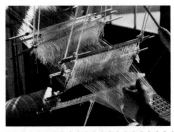

disrespectful (dis ri spekt'fəl) *adj.* To be **disrespectful** is to act without care or thought for others.

rude (rüd') *adj.* A **rude** person says and does things that are not kind.
Cognate (Spanish) **rudo**

famous (fā'məs) *adj.* Someone or something that everyone knows about is **famous**.

skillful (skil'fəl) *adj.* You are **skillful** at something if you can do it very well.

Arachne

READ
To Find Out

What are Arachne's character traits?

Long ago in ancient Greece, there was a girl named Arachne who learned an important lesson. She lived and worked with her father in a small village. Her father dyed wool many different colors. Arachne spun the wool into thin, soft thread. Then she used a **loom** to weave the thread into cloth.

Arachne became very **famous** for her weaving skills. Her fingers moved fast. Her cloth was smooth and her sewing was beautiful. No one had ever seen such skill.

loom machine for making cloth
famous well known

156

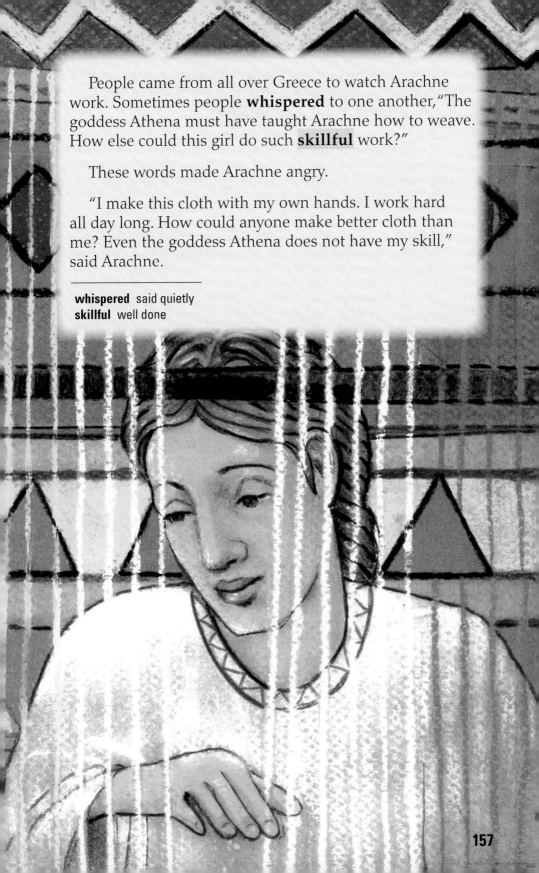

People came from all over Greece to watch Arachne work. Sometimes people **whispered** to one another, "The goddess Athena must have taught Arachne how to weave. How else could this girl do such **skillful** work?"

These words made Arachne angry.

"I make this cloth with my own hands. I work hard all day long. How could anyone make better cloth than me? Even the goddess Athena does not have my skill," said Arachne.

---

whispered said quietly
skillful well done

157

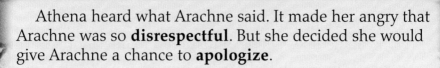

Athena heard what Arachne said. It made her angry that Arachne was so **disrespectful**. But she decided she would give Arachne a chance to **apologize**.

Disguised as an old woman, Athena warned Arachne not to anger the gods. "Foolish girl. How can you say you are equal to the gods? You must speak with Athena and ask her to forgive what you said."

"Old woman, what do you know?" Arachne answered. "If Athena is angry with me, she can talk to me. But I think she is too afraid."

LET'S TALK! Compare what Arachne thinks about her work and what the people think.

disrespectful rude
apologize say sorry
disguised dressed to hide what she really is

READ
To Find Out

Who has greater skill,
Athena or Arachne?

Then Athena removed her disguise and said, "So, Arachne, you think you can weave faster than me. I accept your **challenge**."

Arachne took Athena to one loom and then sat down at the other. The **contest** began. The goddess and the girl worked very fast.

challenge offer of a contest
contest a game or a race to see who can win

159

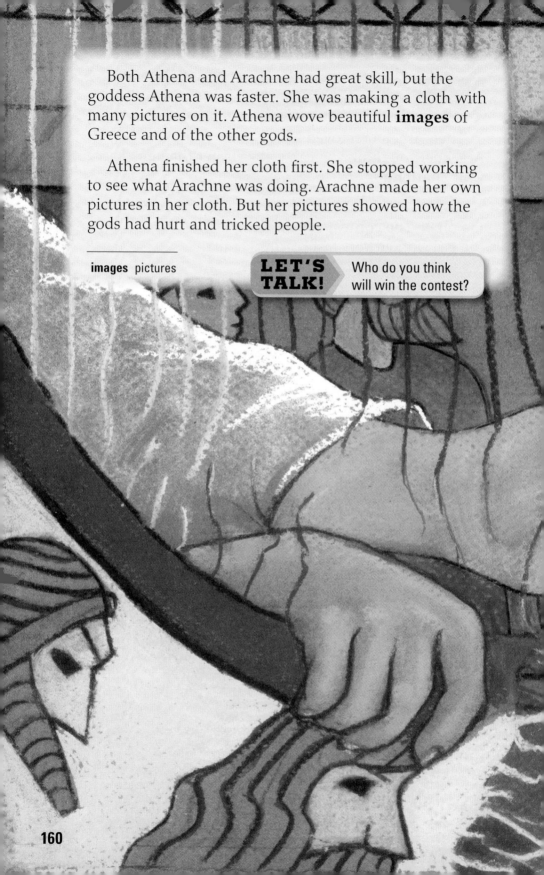

Both Athena and Arachne had great skill, but the goddess Athena was faster. She was making a cloth with many pictures on it. Athena wove beautiful **images** of Greece and of the other gods.

Athena finished her cloth first. She stopped working to see what Arachne was doing. Arachne made her own pictures in her cloth. But her pictures showed how the gods had hurt and tricked people.

images pictures

LET'S TALK! Who do you think will win the contest?

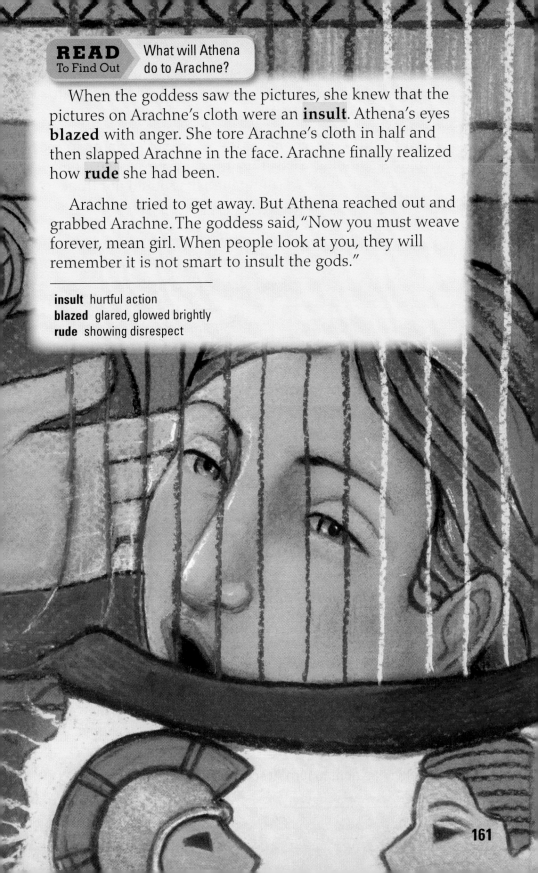

When the goddess saw the pictures, she knew that the pictures on Arachne's cloth were an **insult**. Athena's eyes **blazed** with anger. She tore Arachne's cloth in half and then slapped Arachne in the face. Arachne finally realized how **rude** she had been.

Arachne tried to get away. But Athena reached out and grabbed Arachne. The goddess said, "Now you must weave forever, mean girl. When people look at you, they will remember it is not smart to insult the gods."

insult hurtful action
blazed glared, glowed brightly
rude showing disrespect

Arachne's body **shrank** and her legs became long and thin. Athena had changed Arachne from a girl into a small brown spider!

From that day on, whenever the people of ancient Greece saw spiders spinning webs, they thought of Arachne. They remembered Athena's warning: humans should not think they are equal to the gods.

___

shrank became very small

What Do You Think? Read the following statement. Do you agree or disagree with it? Talk about it with a partner. Make a list of your reasons.

Athena was right to turn Arachne into a spider.

Writing Workshop

Writing a Response to Literature

Writing That Tells About Meaning
An **essay** is a short piece of writing that discusses a topic from the writer's personal point of view. A **response to literature** is an essay in which the writer tells about something he or she has read. The writer looks at the meaning of a text.

Writing Assignment
For this Writing Workshop, you will write a **response to literature** based on a poem you have read. Your essay will explain how the poem answers the question "What makes you who you are?" Write your essay for your classmates and your teacher. They will be your audience.

WRITING PLAN

> Present the thesis, or main idea, of the essay in the first paragraph.

> Organize the essay around three or four ideas that are clear and well thought out.

> Support your ideas with examples from the poem and from real life.

> The last paragraph of your essay should connect back to the thesis.

Writing Model
Read the student model below.

What makes you who you are? Eloise Greenfield explores this in her poem "Daydreamers." She says your daydreams help make you who you are. They show your wishes and hopes. Greenfield explains that when people daydream, they're "thinking up new ways" and "asking new whys." Greenfield thinks daydreams can help you grow and change.

1. **Think of Ideas**
   Take notes as you answer the questions below.
   ○ Which poems explore the question, "What makes you who you are?"
   ○ Which lines in the poems give clear answers to the question?

2. **Choose a Poem**
   Choose a poem to write about. Read the poem aloud and talk about it with a partner.
   ○ Write some words that describe the poem. Think about the poet's main message.
   ○ Write a thesis statement. Your thesis must tell how the poem answers the question. Use this sentence frame to help you:
   The poem "___" by ___ says that ___ make(s) us who we are.

3. **Get Organized**
   Use your notes to complete a word web. Write your thesis statement in the center circle. Fill in the other circles with words or lines from the poem. Choose words or lines that support your thesis.

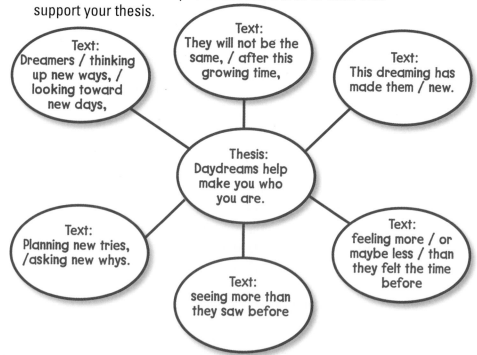

Text:
Dreamers / thinking up new ways, / looking toward new days,

Text:
They will not be the same, / after this growing time,

Text:
This dreaming has made them / new.

Thesis:
Daydreams help make you who you are.

Text:
Planning new tries, /asking new whys.

Text:
seeing more than they saw before

Text:
feeling more / or maybe less / than they felt the time before

Draft

1. **Start Writing**
   Read through your word web, notes, and thesis statement. Use these ideas to help you write.

2. **Add to Your Draft**
   Think about the **themes** in the poem you chose. Then include your thesis statement in the first paragraph of your essay.

> The poem says daydreams make you who you are.

Include words or lines from the poem that **support** your thesis.

> Greenfield explains that people who daydream are "thinking up new ways" and "asking new whys."

Restate your thesis in your last paragraph.

> "Daydreamers" teaches you that daydreams help you grow and change your life.

USE GOOD WRITING TRAITS: WORD CHOICE

When you write, choose words that will help readers clearly understand what you mean. Also choose words that help readers form pictures in their minds and keep readers interested in reading.

A **thesaurus** can help you find the best words to show your meaning. You can look up one word in a thesaurus to find other words with similar meanings. Read the sentence below. Which word makes the writing stronger?

> The poem sparked a thought in my mind.

Revise

Now it's time to revise your draft. This step helps you make your writing better so others will want to read it.

1. **Read Your Essay** Ask yourself these questions:
   - Is the thesis statement clear?
   - What lines from the poem did you use? Are they set off and properly labeled?
   - Do you use complete sentences?

2. **Show Your Essay** Trade drafts with a partner. Answer these questions as you read your partner's essay:
   - Is the thesis statement clear?
   - Is the essay built around three or four clear ideas that are supported by quotes?
   - Does the text make you interested in reading?
   - Is the thesis restated at the end?

3. **Make Your Changes** Talk with your partner to help you decide what changes you need to make. Then revise your essay.

> **Technology** Use the design features of your word processing software to make your text look better. Make your margins wider or narrower, and change the style and size of titles and headings. Remember to indent paragraphs and use quotation marks around lines from the poems.

Edit and Proofread

1. **Proofread Your Essay** Reread your essay. Look for mistakes in capitalization, punctuation, or spelling. Use the proofreading symbols in the chart on page 353 to mark changes.

2. **Check Your Sentences** Did you use complete sentences? Do subjects and verbs agree? Make changes if you need to.

Grammar Focus: Quotations from Poetry

Remember to use quotation marks and slashes for direct quotes. Look at the examples to see how to fix problems.

Problem: It is unclear which words are quoted and which words are the essay writer's.

> People can daydream by holding their bodies still / for a time.

Solution: Place quotation marks before and after the direct quote.

> People can daydream by "holding their bodies still / for a time."

Problem: It is not clear if more than one line from the poem appears in the quote.

> The poem says people "will not be the same after this growing time."

Solution: Use slashes (/) to show where lines begin and end.

> The poem says people "will not be the same / after this growing time."

3. **Make a Final Copy** Make the corrections that you marked. If you are working on the computer, print out the corrected work. If not, rewrite it.

Present

Here are some ways to share your writing.

- Give your essay to your friends to read and ask them for their comments.

- Read the poem and your essay to a partner. Ask your partner to tell you which parts of your essay best supported your thesis.

Speaking, Listening, and Viewing Workshop

Oral Response to Literature

Activity

1. **Connect to Your Writing**
   Deliver an oral response to literature to your classmates. Use the essay you wrote for the Writing Workshop on pages 163–167.

2. **Plan Your Presentation**
   Reread your essay. Mark the parts that you want to include in your presentation. Remember that your essay should have a thesis statement, three or four clear ideas, and direct quotes from the poem. Add music or visuals to add interest to your presentation.

3. **Practice Your Presentation**
   Practice your presentation in front of a mirror. Watch your facial expressions and gestures. Listen to the volume and style of your voice. Practice until you feel ready to give your presentation.

4. **Give Your Presentation**
   - Speak clearly.
   - Change your speaking style to help listeners know your words from the poem's words.
   - Use your voice and your gestures to help listeners remember important points.

Listening To Understand

As you listen to another student's presentation, take notes. Use the sentence frame below to help you better understand what the speaker says.

   - A summary of your idea is ___. Is that correct?

Do It Right!

Illustrated by BROWN

The Boxcar Children

ON MY W
WITH
SESAME ST
I C

Talk About It!

What rules are important at home and at school?

READ
- Classroom Movie Survey
- School Movie Policy
- Parental Notification Form

169

Prepare To Read

Reading Strategy

Draw Conclusions About Meaning and Purpose

A **conclusion** is an opinion you have after thinking about facts. When you **draw conclusions about meaning and purpose**, you ask questions about the text.

To draw conclusions about the **meaning** of a text, ask yourself,

❯ what details or information is in the text?

❯ what is the main idea of the text?

To draw a conclusion about the **purpose** of a text, ask yourself,

❯ why did someone write this?

❯ why is this information important?

As you read, complete the graphic organizer in the *Expressions Practice Book*.

Statement	Agree/Disagree	Why?

Vocabulary for Classroom Movie Survey, School Movie Policy, Parental Notification Form

Read the words and definitions below.

notify (nō′ tə fī) *v.* You **notify** someone when you give that person exact information.
Cognate (Spanish) **notificar**

policy (pä′ lə sē) *n.* A **policy** is a written rule.

rate (rāt′) *v.* When you **rate** something, you judge it.

respectful (ri spekt′ fəl) *adj.* To be **respectful** is to use good manners and kind words.
Cognate (Spanish) **respetuoso(a)**

signature (sig′nə chər) *n.* Your **signature** is how you write your name.

subject (səb′ jikt) *n.* The **subject** is what a book, movie, or speech is mostly about.

survey (sər′ vā) *n.* A **survey** is a list of questions to learn what a group of people think about a product, a problem, or something else.

trust (trəst′) *v.* To believe what someone says is to **trust**.

CLASSROOM

MOVIE SURVEY

READ
To Find Out

How would you answer the questions on this survey?

The teachers at West Middle School show movies and videos in class. Please complete the **survey** to help teachers know how movies help students to learn. Thank you.

1 How often do your teachers show a movie or video in class?

____Every day

____About once a week

____Two to four times a month

____Once or twice a year

2 How many class periods does it usually take to watch the movie or video?

____Less than one class period

____About one full class period

____More than one class period

---

survey a list of questions

3 What kinds of movies have you seen at school? (Check all that apply.)

____ A short movie about health or safety

____ A short movie on a scientific **subject**

____ A short movie about a historical figure or historical period

____ A full-length movie based on a novel or story your class read

4 How helpful is it to watch a movie about what you are learning?

____ Very helpful

____ Not at all helpful

5 How helpful is it to see a movie version of a book you have read?

____ Very helpful

____ Not at all helpful

6 How well do you learn by watching movies compared to reading books?

____ I learn better by watching movies.

____ I learn just as well by watching movies as I do by reading books.

____ I learn better by reading books.

---

subject what the movie is mostly about

7 Do you **trust** information from movies as much as information from books?

_____ I always trust information from movies.

_____ I often trust information from movies.

_____ I sometimes trust information from movies.

_____ I never trust information from movies.

_____ I'm not sure.

8 How do you watch movies in school?

_____ I take notes while I watch.

_____ I pay close attention without taking notes.

_____ I enjoy the movie as if I were in a theater or at home.

_____ I don't watch movies, so it is hard for me to **concentrate**.

9 How often do you watch television or movies outside of school?

_____ Every day

_____ Almost every day

_____ Once in a while

_____ Never

10 How often do you talk with someone at home about the movies you watch in class?

_____ Often

_____ **Rarely**

_____ Never

LET'S TALK! Why do people use surveys?

---

trust believe
concentrate pay close attention or focus
rarely not often

SCHOOL
MOVIE POLICY

READ
To Find Out

What is the school's movie policy?

West School approved this **policy** last January. The school will send a copy of the policy to every student's home.

1. The school will **rate** every movie. Movies on the approved list have a rating of PG or lower.

2. If a teacher plans to show a movie with a higher rating, the teacher must **notify** parents and ask for permission.

3. Students who do not receive permission will leave the classroom during the movie. These students will do other classroom work during that time.

4. Students will be **respectful** while watching the movie. Students will not talk, block the view of other students, or make noise.

LET'S TALK!

Why does the school have a movie policy?

policy rules
rate judge
notify let know
respectful show good manners

175

Parent Notification Form

READ To Find Out — What is the purpose of this form?

Dear Parent,

On January 10, your son or daughter will watch a movie in English class. The movie is *Traveling Down the Path*, and it has a PG13 rating. Please fill out the form below and sign at the bottom. Return the form to your child's English teacher by January 9.

☐ I give permission for _____ to view *Traveling Down the Path* on January 10.

☐ I do not give permission for _____ to view *Traveling Down the Path* on January 10. Please excuse him/her and provide an **alternative** activity.

Signature_____

Date_____

---

notification giving news or information
alternative different choice
signature how a person writes his or her own name

What Do You Think? Do you think your answers to the survey would be like your classmates' answers or different? Compare and contrast your answers to the survey by talking about them in a group. What have you learned about your classmates from your discussion?

Your Idea, My Idea

Talk About It!

What rules help
us stay safe?

READ
- Buckle Up, Pup!
- Riding Without Seatbelts

177

Prepare To Read

Literary Element Argument

An **argument** supports an idea or an opinion. Authors use arguments to get readers to agree with their opinions. Authors may use words that appeal to readers' emotions and logic.

> An **appeal to emotion** tries to make readers feel a certain way.

> An **appeal to logic** tries to get readers to think the argument makes sense.

Practice Read the paragraph. What is the author's argument? Talk about it with a partner.

Swimming is the best kind of exercise. When you swim, your heart becomes stronger and your muscles are firmer. People who swim look great and feel great.

Reading Skill Analyze Figurative Language

Authors use **figurative language** to make descriptions in a text. There are three kinds of figurative language:

> A **simile** uses the words *like* or *as* to compare two unlike things.

> A **metaphor** also compares two unlike things, but does not use *like* or *as*.

> Authors use **personification** to describe animals, objects, or ideas as if they acted like humans.

As you read, complete the graphic organizer in the *Expressions Practice Book*.

Figurative Language	Simile, Metaphor, or Personification	Effect

Vocabulary for Buckle Up, Pup!

Read the words and definitions below.

crate (krāt') *n.* A **crate** is a plastic or wooden container for storing or carrying things.

require (ri kwīr') *v.* When people **require** something, it means you must do it before you can go on or get the next thing.

Cognate (Spanish) **requiera**

harness (här' nəs) *n.* You attach a **harness** with a strap to an animal so that you can control it.

restrained (ri strānd') *v.* When something is tied so it can not move, it is **restrained**.

passengers (pa' sən jərz) *n.* The people who ride in a car, bus, or other transportation are **passengers**.

Cognate (Spanish) **pasajero**

veterinarians (ve te rə ner' ē ənz) *n.* Doctors that help animals are **veterinarians.**

Buckle Up, Pup!

Does your pet ever ride with you in a car? You might take your dog or cat with you on short **errands** and long family trips. Is your pet safe when it rides in your car?

Lawmakers in many states are asking these questions too. Some states may soon **require** dogs to be **restrained** when they ride in cars. Many **veterinarians** agree with the idea.

errands quick trips
require make by force or law
restrained tied down
veterinarians animal doctors

Eyes on the Road

Driving a car is an important job. A driver must pay attention to the road. A dog that is loose in the car could distract the driver. A dog may even block a driver's view. If the pet wants attention from the driver, the driver may forget to pay attention to the road. The pet may cause an **accident**. The pet, the driver, and other people may get hurt. A loose dog in a car is an accident waiting to happen.

Who's in Danger?

Sometimes, a driver must stop quickly. Then the loose pet is in danger. A dog might hit the **dashboard** or fall onto the floor. A dog could be badly hurt if it hits the windshield, a seat, or even other **passengers**.

What Keeps a Pet Safe?

The back seat is the safest place for a dog. Pet owners can put a **safety net** between the front and back seats. The safety net keeps pets from falling into the front seat during a sudden stop or accident.

Some people put their pet in a **crate**. First, they tie the crate down so it cannot move. But a pet is still in danger if an accident happens. The pet will crash like a brick into the walls of the crate. The crate might break open, and then the frightened pet may hurt itself or others.

LET'S TALK! What are some ways to keep pets safe in cars?

---

accident event that happens when people make mistakes
dashboard area beneath windshield for steering wheel and other controls
passengers people in the car
safety net net that holds things in safely
crate box for carrying objects

Attach Your Dog

Some people restrain their dog with a **harness**. The harness **attaches** to a seatbelt. The dog can sit or lie on the car seat, but it cannot jump between the seats. The harness keeps the dog safe in case the car gets into an accident.

Have you ever seen a dog hang its head out the car window? Dogs like the wind, but sometimes the wind blows dirt in the dog's eye. The dirt is like a flying **needle** that can hurt the pet's eye. A harness keeps the pet inside so it will not hang its head out and the wind will not hurt it.

Is a dog safe in the back of a pickup truck? A loose dog can jump from the truck and get badly injured. Then another **vehicle** might hit the dog. Some pet owners who drive pickup trucks want to be sure their pet is safe. They attach a harness in the back of the truck, and make sure their dog cannot jump out.

---

harness straps to control an animal
attaches connects or joins to
needle a slender tool with a very sharp point
vehicle car or other transportation that people ride in

182

Who Is in Charge?

Drivers are **responsible** for their pets. Drivers must keep their pets safe. They must help other drivers stay safe too. If drivers restrain their pets in the car, they will be responsible drivers. Their pets will be thankful too!

---

responsible in charge

What Do You Think? What does the author of "Buckle Up, Pup!" think about dogs in cars? Do you agree with the author? Explain your answer to a partner.

Vocabulary for Riding Without Seatbelts

Read the words and definitions below.

adopt (ə däpt') *v.* When you bring a new person or animal to your home to live as part of your family, you **adopt** the person or animal.
Cognate (Spanish) **adoptar**

shelters (shel' tərz) *n.* **Shelters** are where you find dogs and cats that need new homes.

leashes (lēsh' əz) *n.* If you hold straps or ropes that you tied to animals, you are holding **leashes**.

thrilled (thrild') *adj.* When you are very excited, you are **thrilled**.

liberty (li' bər tē) *n.* When you are free, you have **liberty**.
Cognate (Spanish) **libertad**

training (trā' nin) *v.* When you teach your dog to sit or to stay, you are **training** it.

obedient (ō be dē' ənt) *adj.* A dog that does what its owners tell it to do is an **obedient** dog.

trap (trap') *v.* A person or thing that wants you to stay could **trap** you inside a place.
Cognate (Spanish) **trampa**

Riding Without Seatbelts

READ To Find Out

Why should dogs be able to ride without seatbelts?

Do dogs love to ride in cars? Of course, you do not know for sure what a dog thinks and feels. Yet, it is easy to see that most dogs are **thrilled** when they go for a ride. They stick their heads out the windows and open their mouths to breathe in the air. Their ears flap in the wind like wings. A dog is a best friend to its owner. A dog should have the freedom to enjoy a car ride.

---

thrilled very excited

185

Laws for Dogs

Some lawmakers want to take away a dog's **liberty**. They think that dogs should have to follow the same laws as people. These lawmakers want dogs to be tied down in the car. They want dogs to wear special harnesses that attach to seatbelts. If dogs have to wear a harness, they won't be able to move around. They also won't enjoy the ride if they can't put their heads out the window.

LET'S TALK! What do lawmakers want to do?

---
liberty freedom

Pet Owners and the Law

Pet laws exist now. Some laws say that owners must put **leashes** on dogs. Other laws say that dogs must have **licenses**. Those laws are enough. The law should not tell owners to put harnesses on dogs in cars. Dogs should be free in cars.

Pet owners spend money on food, supplies, and medical care for the animals they love. They spend even more money on licenses, leashes, and collars. This law would force owners to buy more **equipment**. Pet owners do not need to spend more. Maybe more people would **adopt** pets from **shelters** if the people were not worried about spending so much money.

---

leashes something to restrain an animal
licenses fees paid to use or own something
equipment tools for doing something
adopt take home
shelters places for pets without homes

187

Pet Owners Must Be Responsible

Pet owners are responsible for **training** their pets. Dogs will be **obedient** if the owners train them. The law should not punish pets if a few owners do not train their pets. The law should let pets be free inside of cars.

How do most dogs act in a moving car? Most will just lie down and go to sleep. If a car ride excites some dogs, then those dogs should wear harnesses.

Harnesses for dogs might do more harm than good. What would happen to a harnessed dog in an accident? If a car gets in an accident, a harness could **trap** a dog inside. What if the people in the car were injured? A dog in a harness could not go for help.

Lawmakers have more important problems. Pets are not an important problem. Some pet owners will buy harnesses, but some do not want them. The owners can decide what is best. The owners care the most about their pets and they will make the right choice.

---

training teaching a dog to behave
obedient well-behaved
trap to get stuck

What Do You Think? Look back at the two articles. Have you changed your mind about dogs riding in cars? Talk with a partner about which article you agree with. Give two reasons from the article to support your answer.

Small Hunters in a Big World

Talk About It!

What do you think about spiders?

READ
- Tarantulas!
- Spiders of North America

Prepare To Read

Literary Element **Thesis**

The **thesis** is the main idea of an essay.

❯ Sometimes the thesis is stated at the beginning of an essay.

❯ Sometimes you must use information in the essay to figure out the thesis.

A thesis also tells you what is important to the author. As you read, ask yourself: "What does the author want me to understand?"

Practice Read the paragraph. What is the thesis?

> Cities are different and interesting. Some cities are by the ocean. Some are in the mountains. Many cities have tall buildings. Other cities have many bridges.

- -

Reading Skill **Analyze Voice**

When you **analyze voice**, you look at the way the author writes. You think about the words the author uses. You think about how long the sentences are. Analyzing voice can help you understand the mood of the essay. As you read, ask yourself:

❯ why did the author use these words?

❯ why did the author write the sentences this way?

As you read, complete the graphic organizer in the *Expressions Practice Book*.

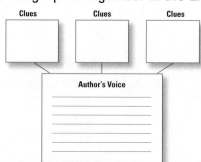

Vocabulary for Tarantulas!

Read the words and definitions below.

disease (di zēz') *n.* A certain kind of sickness is a **disease**.

paralyzes (per' ə lī zez) *v.* If something makes you unable to move, it **paralyzes** you.
Cognate (Spanish) **paralizar**

fangs (fangz') *n.* Long, sharp teeth are **fangs**.

prey (prā') *n.* When animals hunt for **prey**, they hunt for other animals.
Cognate (Spanish) **presa**

hiss (his') *v.* To **hiss** is to make a sound like air leaking out of a tire.

senses (sen' sez) *n.* When you see, taste, hear, touch, or smell something, you are using your **senses**.
Cognate (Spanish) **sentidos**

liquid (li' kwəd) *n.* A **liquid** is wet and flows like water.
Cognate (Spanish) **liquido**

venom (ve' nəm) *n.* **Venom** is a poison.
Cognate (Spanish) **veneno**

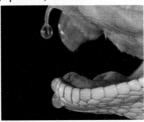

Tarantulas!

READ To Find Out

Are tarantulas really killers?

Did you know that tarantulas are the largest spiders? Some tarantulas are as big as your hand. They may grow as large as a soccer ball.

You can imagine why tarantulas appear in scary movies. Tarantulas can be killers. These big, hairy spiders have eight eyes and two large **fangs**. Their teeth have **venom** that can kill an enemy.

Yet, tarantulas must fight to survive. They do not see well, even though they have eight eyes. They rely on other **senses** to live.

---

fangs sharp pointy teeth
venom poison
senses sight, taste, touch, hearing, smell

192

Tarantula Tales

People around the world tell stories of tarantulas. One story comes from Taranto, Italy. People there believed that a bite from a tarantula caused a strange **disease**. Anyone with the disease would jump wildly and make strange noises. The people made up a jumping dance to keep the sickness away. They called it the *tarantella*, or spider dance. People still dance the *tarantella* for fun.

Old stories made tarantulas sound scary, but tarantulas do not hunt or kill people for food. In fact, tarantulas rarely bite people. They hunt other **prey**. These giant spiders will hunt and kill small insects like beetles and grasshoppers.

disease illness
prey the animal that is hunted

> **LET'S TALK!** Why did people begin to dance the spider dance?

Eight-Legged Hunter

A tarantula uses its sense of touch when it hunts at night. It can feel a breeze with its hairy body. It can also feel the air move when insects are crawling nearby. The tarantula gets close to an insect and grabs it. It quickly bites the insect with its fangs. The fangs fill with venom. The venom goes into the insect's body. The venom **paralyzes** the insect so it cannot get away.

The tarantula cannot eat the insect yet. The tarantula does not eat solid food. First, it must turn the inside of the insect into **liquid**. The fangs squirt juices into the insect. The juices make the insect soft on the inside. The tarantula then sucks out the liquid. It's like insect soup!

A Spider's Weapons

A tarantula uses different parts of its body to protect itself. For example, it can **hiss** to scare an enemy. It rubs its hairy legs together to make the sound.

A tarantula will also make its hairs fly into the air. The hairs hit an enemy and cause itching and burning. Hair may not look as scary as fangs, but it is good protection!

---

paralyzes make unable to move
liquid like water
weapons any means of harming someone or something
hiss to make a sound like air coming out of a tire

Popular Pets

Many people have tarantulas as pets. People like them because they are quiet and do not make messes. Some people just enjoy watching them. If you stop at a pet store, you can see them for yourself. Would you want the largest spider in the world as your pet?

---

popular liked by many people

What Do You Think? What is your idea of a tarantula? Draw it as a pet or in nature. Describe your picture to a partner.

Vocabulary for Spiders of North America

Read the words and definitions below.

adult (ə dəlt′) *n.* An **adult** is a full-grown person or animal.
Cognate (Spanish) **adulto**

funnel (fə′ nəl) *n.* A **funnel** is the shape of a cone. It is wide at one end, and narrow at the other end.

segments (seg′ mənts) *n.* **Segments** are parts of a whole thing.
Cognate (Spanish) **segmentos**

silk (silk′) *n.* **Silk** is soft, thin thread.

sticky (sti′ kē) *adj.* Something that acts like glue and makes two things stay tightly together is **sticky**.

trap (trap′) *v.* Catching another animal is to **trap**.
Cognate (Spanish) **trampa**

venomous (ve′ nə məs) *adj.* An animal that uses poison as a weapon is **venomous**.
Cognate (Spanish) **venenoso(a)**

webs (webz′) *n.* **Webs** are thin structures made by spiders.

Spiders of North America

READ To Find Out — How are spiders different from ins

Webs, Traps, and Bites

Did you know that spiders aren't insects? They are arachnids. You can find many kinds of spiders in North America.

Spiders are different from insects because they have eight legs, while insects have only six. A spider's body has two **segments** but an insect has three.

Spiders are known for making **webs**. A spider can produce **silk** and spin it into threads to make a web. A spider web is **sticky**. Insects fly into the web and get stuck. Then the spider has food to eat.

---

segments different parts of a whole object
webs the structures made by spiders
silk soft, thin thread
sticky makes things stay together

Deadly Traps

Some spiders use their silk in other ways to **trap** an insect. The trapdoor spider lives in a small hole in the ground. The spider makes a kind of a door over the hole with its silk and dirt. When an insect walks by, the spider pushes through the door, grabs the insect, and eats it.

Funnel spiders build webs shaped like a **funnel**. The web looks like an ice-cream cone. It has a wide opening on top. It narrows to a point on the bottom. Insects that crawl into the web get stuck at the bottom.

A Bite to Be Afraid Of?

Has a spider ever bitten you? The bite probably did not hurt for long. Almost all spiders are **venomous**. But very few spiders have venom strong enough to hurt people. The black widow lives in the United States. The **adult** female is dangerous to humans. Black widows and most other spiders bite only when someone touches them. It's best to just look at them!

---

trap catch
funnel an object that is wide at one end, and narrow at the other end
venomous poisonous
adult full grown person or animal

What Do You Think? What did you think about spiders before you read the article? What do you think about spiders now? Talk about it in a small group.

I used to think that spiders ____.

Now I think that spiders ____.

Big and Small LESSONS

Prepare To Read

Literary Element Fable

A **fable** is a short story that teaches a
lesson. Fables are stories that people
tell again and again.

> The lesson in a fable is called a **moral**.
>   Morals are lessons about right and wrong.

> Animal characters in fables talk and act
>   like people.

Practice Read the paragraph. What tells
you that this is a fable?

The ant saved food all summer while the grasshopper played his
fiddle. When winter came, the grasshopper had no food. The ant
had food because he worked all summer. The ant knew that hard
work makes things easy later on.

Reading Strategy Make Generalizations About Characters

When you **make generalizations about characters**, first you think about
what characters do and say. Then you look at how they act. Making
generalizations can help you find the moral of a fable. As you read,
complete the graphic organizer in the *Expressions Practice Book*.

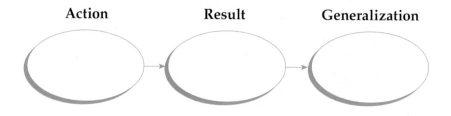

Action   Result   Generalization

amazed (ə māzd') *adj.* When you are **amazed**, you cannot believe what you have seen or heard

connects (kə nekts') *v.* When something **connects**, it joins with something else.
Cognate (Spanish) **conectar**

forest (for' əst) *n.* A **forest** is an area with many trees.

grateful (grāt' fəl) *adj.* When you are **grateful**, you are thankful.
Cognate (Spanish) **agradecido(a)**

healthy (hel' thē) *adj.* A **healthy** person is not sick and feels well.

servants (sər' vənts) *n.* **Servants** work in a house to care for the people who live there.
Cognate (Spanish) **sirvientes**

The Wolf in the Forest

The Dog in the HOUSE

Based on a story by Aesop

Aesop was a storyteller who told fables in ancient Greece.

READ
To Find Out

Why is the wolf so hungry?

There once was a wolf that lived in the **forest**. The wolf was a good hunter. She had always been able to find food. But now, it was harder and harder to find food in the forest. The wolf went to sleep hungry and woke up feeling hungry. She became so **skinny** that her ribs showed.

One day, while she was searching for food, the wolf met a dog from the village. The dog was **plump** and **healthy**.

"Excuse me, but why are you so healthy?" asked the wolf. "It has been hard for me to find food in the forest."

forest an area with many trees
skinny thin
plump fat
healthy not sick

"I never have to find my food," said the dog. "My master feeds me well. His **servants** feed me food from the kitchen every day. All I have to do is watch over the house at night and bark at **strangers**."

The wolf was **amazed**. "Do you think I could find a family to live with?" she asked.

"I can find a family for you. Just follow me," said the dog. The dog walked ahead with his head high. The **grateful** wolf followed.

Just then, the wolf saw something around the dog's neck.

---

servants people who work for and wait on other people
strangers people you do not know
amazed surprised
grateful thankful for something

"Excuse me, but what is that thing around your neck?" the wolf asked.

"That is my **collar**," said the dog. "My master **connects** it to a **chain**."

"A chain!" cried the wolf.

"Yes, a chain," said the dog. "All dogs are chained at night so we will not run away. Now come along!" He turned and walked toward the village.

"You cannot expect me to wear a chain. No, thank you," said the wolf. "I would rather be hungry in the forest than eat with a chain around my neck."

---

collar a band of material worn around the neck
connects to become joined together
chain metal links used to keep something or someone from moving

LESSON
It is better to have less and be free than have more and be chained.

What Do You Think? Reread the lesson at the end of the story. Do you agree or disagree with it? Discuss your opinion with a partner.

Vocabulary for Greek Poetry

Read the words and definitions below.

attack (ə tak') *v.* To use violence against someone is to **attack**.
Cognate (Spanish) **atacar**

celebrate (se' lə brāt) *v.* When you do something special for a certain person or event, you **celebrate**.
Cognate (Spanish) **celebrar**

courage (kər' ij) *adj.* If you have **courage**, you are not afraid to do something dangerous.
Cognate (Spanish) **coraje**

enormous (i nor' məs) *adj.* Something that is very large is **enormous**.
Cognate (Spanish) **enorme**

heroes (hir' ōz) *n.* **Heroes** are people who do great things that help others.
Cognate (Spanish) **héroes**

intelligence (in te' lə jəns) *n.* You use your **intelligence** to solve problems.
Cognate (Spanish) **inteligencia**

models (mä' dəlz) *n.* **Models** are examples of how to do or make something.
Cognate (Spanish) **modelos**

save (sāv') *v.* When you **save** something, you keep it safe from danger or harm.
Cognate (Spanish) **salvar**

READ To Find Out ▶ Where do ideas for stories come from?

Have you ever listened to a story and said, "That sounds like something I've heard before"? Well, you may have heard it before. Many writers use stories and poems they have read as **models** for their own writing.

The earliest Greek stories were long poems called epics. The poems were about **heroes**. Heroes are people with great strength and **courage**. The poet Homer wrote the first great epics in the seventh century B.C.

---

models examples
heroes people who do great things
courage not having fear when there is danger

THE ILIAD

Homer wrote the *Iliad* and the *Odyssey*. People still read these two epic poems today. They are stories about a real war between Greece and the city of Troy.

In the *Iliad*, a prince of Troy **kidnaps** the Queen of Sparta, which is a city in ancient Greece. That makes the Greeks very angry. They **attack** Troy and start a war. After ten years of war, the Greeks make a new plan to attack the city of Troy. They build an **enormous** wooden horse. The horse has space inside where many Greek soldiers can hide. Other soldiers take the horse to the city gates. The people of Troy think that the Greeks have stopped fighting and are giving them the horse as a gift.

LET'S TALK! Describe the Greek's plan to attack Troy.

---

kidnaps takes someone by force
attack using force to hurt someone or something
enormous very large

207

READ
To Find Out

Who was a hero
to the Greeks?

The people of Troy take the **giant** horse into the city
and close the gates. They **celebrate** because they think
the war is over. When the people of Troy are asleep, the
Greek soldiers come out from inside the horse and
open the city gates. The other Greek soldiers come
in and attack Troy.

giant   very big; large
celebrate   have a party and give thanks

A HERO FOR ALL GREEKS

The *Odyssey* tells the story of Odysseus, a hero in the war with Troy. The poem is about his **journey** home after the war. The trip takes ten years, and it's full of danger. Today we use the word *odyssey* to mean a long trip with many **adventures**.

journey trip
adventures exciting activities

Odysseus is a very **intelligent** hero. It was his idea to build the Trojan horse. On his long trip home, he uses his **intelligence** to help **save** himself and the other soldiers who are traveling with him.

The Greeks thought of the *Iliad* and the *Odyssey* as more than just stories. Homer's poems taught many things. They taught about intelligence, strength, and courage. They taught that friendship is important. That is why the Greek people liked stories about heroes like Odysseus.

---

intelligent smart
intelligence being able to learn or solve problems
save to free from danger

What Do You Think? The ancient Greeks used stories and fables to teach lessons. Think of a lesson you learned from a story or fable you know. Tell the fable and the lesson to your partner. Use the sentence frames below.

I know a story about___.

I learned___from this story.

The Right to Play

Talk About It!

How can people choose to act when they are not treated fairly?

READ
- Jackie Robinson
- The Baseball Diamond

Literary Element Text Structure

Text structure is the way a writer organizes ideas. A writer may put the ideas in time order. This is called **chronological order**. To identify chronological order in a text

❯ look for dates of events.

❯ look for clue words like *first*, *then*, *next*, and *last*.

Practice Read the paragraph. What words tell you the text structure is chronological order?

> After school, I had to do my chores. First, I took the dog for a walk. Next, I cleaned my room and made my bed. Finally, I helped my sister wash the dishes.

Reading Strategy Monitor Comprehension

When you **monitor comprehension**, you make sure you understand the text. If you don't understand what you are reading, follow these steps:

❯ stop reading;

❯ ask yourself what just happened;

❯ try to tell what happened in your own words;

❯ read the text again until you understand it.

As you read, complete the graphic organizer in the *Expressions Practice Book*. Look for major events in the text, and record when they happened, and what the event was.

Jackie Robinson	
Date	Event

Vocabulary for Jackie Robinson

Read the words and definitions below.

celebration (se' lə brā shən) *n.* People gathering to honor someone's birthday are at a birthday **celebration**.
Cognate (Spanish) **celebración**

equal (ē' kwəl) *adj.* When two things are exactly the same in some way, they are **equal**.
Cognate (Spanish) **igual**

interview (in' tər vyü) *n.* An **interview** is a meeting with two people. One person asks questions and the other person answers.

journalist (jər' nə list) *n.* The job of a **journalist** is to write articles for newspapers or magazines.

league (lēg') *n.* If you play a sport in a league, you play games against other teams in the **league**.
Cognate (Spanish) **liga**

pitchers (pi' chərz) *n.* Players who throw balls to batters are **pitchers**.

public (pə' blik) *adj.* Something that can be used by all people, such as a park or bus, is **public**.
Cognate (Spanish) **público(a)**

segregation (se gri gā' shən) *n.* A country that forces certain groups of people to be separate, forces them to live under **segregation**.
Cognate (Spanish) **segregación**

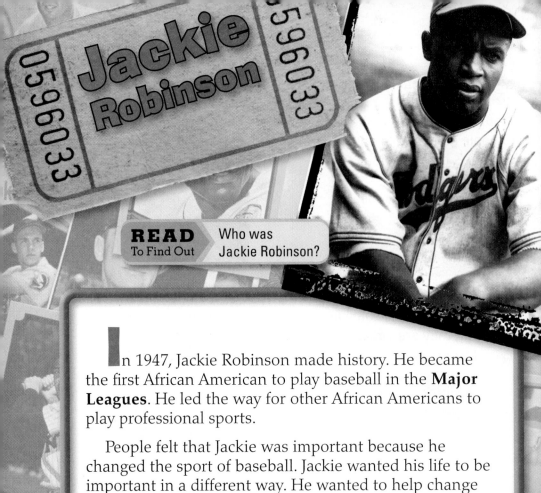

Jackie Robinson

READ To Find Out Who was Jackie Robinson?

In 1947, Jackie Robinson made history. He became the first African American to play baseball in the **Major Leagues**. He led the way for other African Americans to play professional sports.

People felt that Jackie was important because he changed the sport of baseball. Jackie wanted his life to be important in a different way. He wanted to help change people's lives. In his lifetime, Jackie gave hope to **millions** of people.

Jackie Roosevelt Robinson was born in Cairo, Georgia, on January 31, 1919. His mother, Mallie, moved her family to Pasadena, California, in search of a better life. In Georgia, the family had lived under **segregation**. **Public** places were separated for blacks and whites under segregation. African American people could not eat in some restaurants. They had to sit in separate sections in movie theaters. And, they could swim in the public pool only on certain days.

Major Leagues the top league in baseball
millions 1,000,000s
segregation different groups of people that must live separately
public for the use of all people

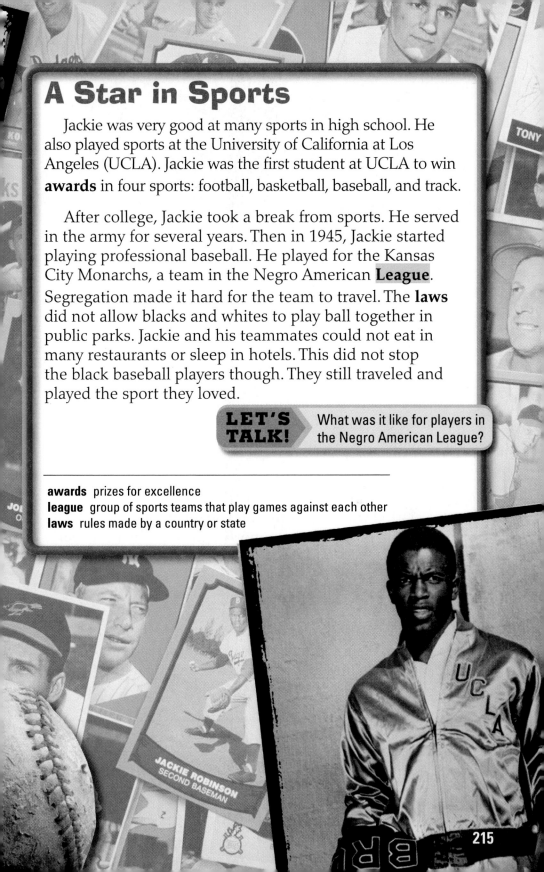

A Star in Sports

Jackie was very good at many sports in high school. He also played sports at the University of California at Los Angeles (UCLA). Jackie was the first student at UCLA to win **awards** in four sports: football, basketball, baseball, and track.

After college, Jackie took a break from sports. He served in the army for several years. Then in 1945, Jackie started playing professional baseball. He played for the Kansas City Monarchs, a team in the Negro American **League**. Segregation made it hard for the team to travel. The **laws** did not allow blacks and whites to play ball together in public parks. Jackie and his teammates could not eat in many restaurants or sleep in hotels. This did not stop the black baseball players though. They still traveled and played the sport they loved.

LET'S TALK! What was it like for players in the Negro American League?

---

awards prizes for excellence
league group of sports teams that play games against each other
laws rules made by a country or state

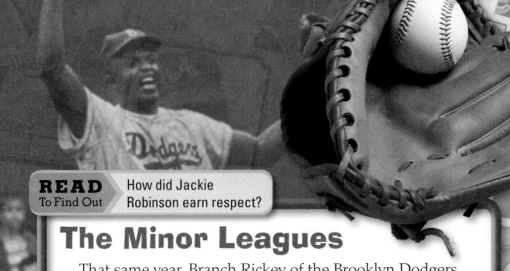

READ
To Find Out

How did Jackie Robinson earn respect?

The Minor Leagues

That same year, Branch Rickey of the Brooklyn Dodgers was looking for an African American player to join the Major Leagues. Rickey knew that Jackie Robinson was a great ballplayer. He also knew that fans were not used to African Americans and whites playing together. Many fans would not like Jackie. Would he get angry if fans called him names?

Rickey called Jackie in for an **interview**. Rickey explained that fans might get mad if an African American player joined the team. "I'm looking for a ballplayer with **guts** enough not to fight back," Rickey said.

Jackie promised to be that player. On October 23, 1945, Jackie started with the **minor league** team for the Brooklyn Dodgers. He played in the minor leagues for the next year and a half.

Into the Majors

On April 15, 1947, Jackie Robinson put on a Brooklyn Dodgers team shirt with number 42. He walked on the field to play his first Major League baseball game.

---

interview   a meeting for asking questions of a person
guts   bravery
minor league   where baseball players train to get to the Major Leagues

This was the first time an African American person would play in the Major Leagues. One **journalist** wrote that the game would change baseball forever. It would change the ways Americans thought. That day, many fans yelled at Robinson. **Pitchers** threw the ball close to his head. Jackie kept his promise to Branch Rickey. He did not fight back.

During Jackie's time with the Brooklyn Dodgers, the team won six National League championships. They also won the World Series in 1955. Fans came to respect Jackie for his skill and sportsmanship.

Jackie stopped playing baseball in 1957. He decided to spend the rest of his life speaking about **equal** rights for all Americans. Jackie Robinson died on October 24, 1972. He was 53 years old.

A Major League Celebration

On April 15, 1997, the Los Angeles Dodgers had a **celebration** for Jackie Roosevelt Robinson. They decided that no other baseball player would ever wear the number 42 Dodgers team shirt again.

journalist a person who writes for a newspaper
pitchers players who throw the ball to the batter
equal the same
celebration an event to honor someone

What Do You Think? Jackie Robinson was the first African American baseball player in the Major Leagues. Read the statement below. With a partner, think of examples from the text that support the statement.

It is always hard to be the first at something.

Vocabulary for The Baseball Diamond

Read the words and definitions below.

base (bās′) *n.* A **base** is one of four stations in a baseball field that must be passed to score a point.
Cognate (Spanish) **base**

club (kləb′) *n.* A **club** is a group of people with similar interests who share activities together.
Cognate (Spanish) **club**

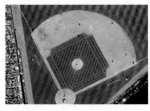

diamond (dī′ ə mənd) *n.* A **diamond** is a shape with four sides.

foul line (fau′ əl līn′) *n.* A foul line is one of two lines on each side of a baseball field used to tell if a ball is in or out of play.

home plate (hōm′ plāt′) *n.* **Home plate** is where the batter stands and what must be touched to score points during a baseball game.

mound (maund′) *n.* The **mound** is where the pitcher stands to throw the baseball.

pastime (pas′ tīm) *n.* A **pastime** is an activity that people do for fun.
Cognate (Spanish) **pasatiempo**

popular (pä′ pyə lər) *n.* Something is **popular** when many people like it.
Cognate (Spanish) **popular**

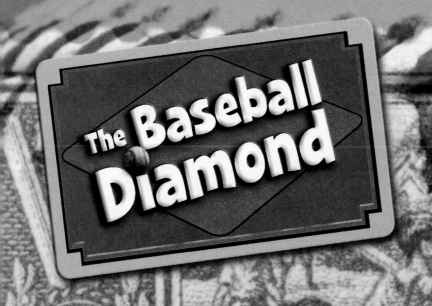

The Baseball Diamond

READ To Find Out — What was it like to play baseball at first?

Many people in the United States love baseball. People call this sport "the National **Pastime**" because so many people like to play and watch the game. How much do you know about how the game began?

Americans first started playing baseball in the early 1800s. Back then, baseball did not have the rules it has today. People in different neighborhoods would use different rules. As baseball became more **popular**, people wanted the rules to be the same for everyone. In 1845, Alexander Cartwright invented the baseball **diamond**. Soon, all baseball games were played on a diamond. Cartwright also helped start the New York Knickerbocker Base Ball **Club**. He and his team made the rules that baseball players use today.

---

pastime a fun activity
popular something a lot of people like
diamond a shape with four sides
club group of people who meet to share an activity

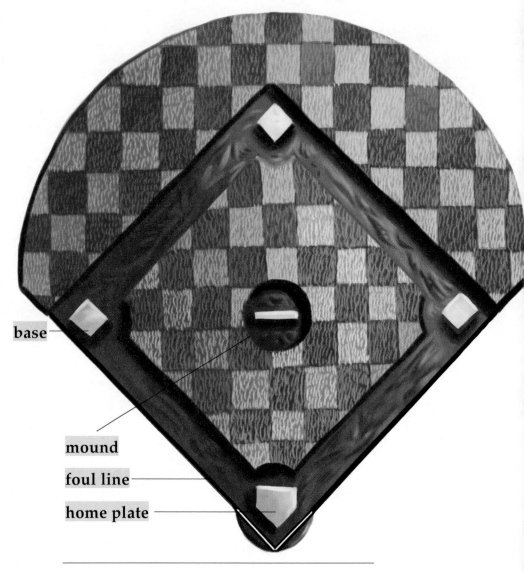

base

mound

foul line

home plate

home plate where the batters stand
base one of four corners of a baseball diamond
foul line line that marks where balls can land and be in play
mound small hill

What Do You Think? What is your favorite sport or activity? Draw a picture of what you like to do or where you play the game. Add labels to your drawing. Then share your drawing with a partner.

Writing Workshop

Writing a Persuasive Essay

Writing That Takes a Position
Think about the question, "What's fair and what's not?" When something is unfair, how do you try to make it better? You probably say what is wrong. Then you give your reasons. When you take a position, you try to **persuade** others to think the way you do.

Writing Assignment
For this Writing Workshop, you will write a **persuasive essay**. You will explain a **problem** and propose a **solution**. You will write your essay for your classmates and your teacher. They will be your audience.

> ### ▶ WRITING PLAN
>
> - ▶ State a clear position in the introduction.
> - ▶ Present your reasons for your position in the best order.
>
> - ▶ People might disagree with your position. Try to respond to their ideas.
> - ▶ Conclude your essay by restating your main points and asking readers to take action.

Writing Model
Read the student model below.

Last Friday, Dustin Barnes tripped and sprained his ankle. He had to wear large dress shoes as part of a dress code. Those shoes are dangerous. If Dustin had been allowed to wear gym shoes, he would not have hurt himself. The school dress code should be changed so students can wear any kind of shoes.

Prewrite

1. Gather Ideas

To get started on your persuasive essay, think about things you know that are unfair. List some unfair situations that you know about and ask the following questions:

- What is unfair about each problem?
- Do I feel strongly about any of these problems?
- Can I do anything about these problems?

2. Choose a Topic

Read your notes. Then choose a problem that you care about strongly. Make an idea tree that shows the problem along with reasons the problem is bad. Then list a solution and reasons that the solution can work well.

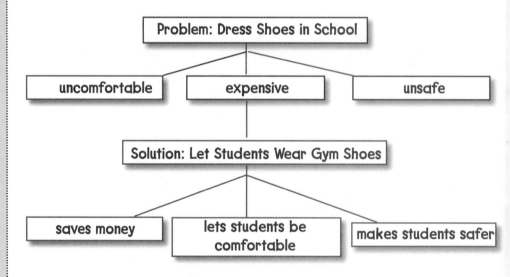

3. Get Organized

Write a sentence that states your argument. This is called a **position statement**. Make a list of details that support your position. These are called **pros**. Then write a list of details that might be bad things about your position. These are called **cons**. Use your position statement and your list of pros and cons to write an **outline** for your essay.

Draft

1. **Start Writing**
   Use your idea tree and outline to help you write your persuasive essay.

2. **Add to Your Draft**
   State your **argument** clearly in the first paragraph.

> The school should let students wear the shoes that they want to wear.

For each paragraph in the **body** of the essay, write a topic sentence that supports the argument.

> The dress code is unfair because it makes students uncomfortable.

End the essay with a possible **solution** to the problem and ask readers to take action.

> Write to the principal to change the dress code so students can wear any kind of shoes.

USE GOOD WRITING TRAITS: VOICE
The words you use and the way you use them is called **voice**. Voice is how an author shows feelings about a topic. Voice helps readers stay interested in reading.

Read the following example. Pay attention to how the words show emotion.

> Wearing dress shoes all day crushes your feet.

Read your essay aloud. Ask yourself: Does the reader get to know the real me?

Revise

Now it's time to revise your draft. This step helps you make your writing better, so others will want to read it.

1. **Read Your Essay** Ask yourself these questions:
   - Does it present both a problem and solution?
   - Do the problem and solution have reasons to support them?
   - Are the problem and solution summarized by the end of the essay?

2. **Show Your Essay** Trade drafts with a partner. Answer these questions as you read your partner's essay.
   - Is the problem stated clearly and with reasons?
   - Is the solution presented with reasons supporting it?
   - Do the reasons for the solution make sense?
   - Does the essay answer the arguments other people might have?

3. **Make Your Changes** Talk with your partner to help you decide what changes you need to make. Then revise your draft.

> **Technology** Use the design features of your word processing software to make your text look better. Use fonts and text features to add **emphasis** to important details in your argument. Create charts and lists that might help convince readers that your position is correct.

Edit and Proofread

1. **Proofread Your Essay** Reread your essay. Look for mistakes in capitalization, punctuation, or spelling. Use the proofreading symbols chart on page 353 to mark changes.

2. **Check Your Sentences** Are all your details easy to read and understand? Is all your information true? Make changes if you need to.

Grammar Focus: Parallel Structure

In your sentences, make sure that you write similar words and phrases with the same patterns. This is called **parallel structure**.

Problem: The ideas in a sentence are similar, but do not appear in the same way.

Example A:

The shoes are painful and we are put in danger by the shoes.

Solution: Create similar **sentence structure**.

The shoes are painful and dangerous.

Example B:

The dress code is unfair, uncomfortable, and a bore.

Solution: Make sure that the items in a list are all the same part of speech.

The dress code is unfair, uncomfortable, and boring.

3. **Make a Final Copy** Make the corrections that you marked. Print out or rewrite the corrected work.

Present

Here are some ways to share your writing.

○ Give your essay to friends to read and ask them for comments.

○ Imagine that your friends support the opposite view presented in the essay. Have them list the points in the essay that best convince them of your argument.

▣ Speaking, Listening, and Viewing Workshop

Persuasive Speech

Activity

1. **Connect to Your Writing**
   Deliver a persuasive speech to your classmates. Use the persuasive essay you wrote for the Writing Workshop on pages 221–225.

2. **Plan Your Speech**
   Reread your essay. Mark the parts you want to include in your speech. Your speech needs a clear, well-supported argument about a problem and it should offer a solution. Write the reasons for each on note cards.

3. **Practice Your Speech**
   Practice your speech several times in front of a mirror. Watch your facial expressions and gestures. Listen to the volume and style of your voice. Practice until you feel ready to give your speech.

4. **Deliver Your Speech**
   - Speak clearly.
   - Speed up or slow down while speaking to emphasize important ideas.

Listening to Learn

As you listen to another student's speech, take notes. What did you like about that speech? Did you think the reasons and solution were realistic? Share your ideas with the student. Use the sentence frames below.

- I agree/disagree with your point about ___ because ___. Can you give more evidence for your support?
- I can summarize your speech this way: ___. Is that correct?

Love What You Do

READ Three Essays:
- A Longer, Smarter Vacation
- Ted the Iguana
- Hurray for Artists!

227

Prepare To Read

Literary Element | Author's Purpose

Authors write for different reasons. They write to entertain, to inform, to persuade, or to describe. They may describe people, things, and emotions. When you know an **author's purpose**, you will better understand the author's message. To find the author's purpose, ask yourself:

➤ What is the main reason the author wrote the selection?

➤ What does the author's purpose help me learn about the text?

Practice Read the paragraph. What is the author's purpose? Talk about it with a partner.

> Tomorrow is the field trip to the zoo. Please remember to wear comfortable shoes and bring a sack lunch. The bus leaves at 9:00 a.m.

Reading Skill | Analyze Tone

You can tell how a person feels from the sound of his or her voice. When you **analyze tone** in a text, you look for words and details that show how the author feels about the topic or subject. The feeling the author shows is the tone of the story or article. As you read, complete the graphic organizer in the *Expressions Practice Book*.

Words and Details in Text	How The Words and Details Show the Author's Tone

Vocabulary for Three Essays

Read the words and definitions below.

confident (kän' fə dent) *adj.* When you feel **confident**, you feel sure about what you say and do.

planet (pla' nət) *n.* A **planet** is a large object that moves around the sun. Earth is a planet.
Cognate (Spanish) **planeta**

crops (kröps') *n.* **Crops** are plants that people grow for food.

spikes (spīks') *n.* **Spikes** are long, thin objects with sharp points.

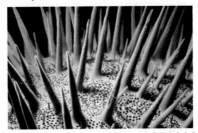

farm (färm') *n.* A **farm** is an area of land where plants are grown and animals are raised for food.

teams (tēmz') *n.* **Teams** are groups of people who work together for the same reason.

painting (pān' tiŋ) *v.* You are **painting** when you are making a picture with paints.
Cognate (Spanish) **pintura**

vacation (vā kā' shən) *n.* A **vacation** is free time when people do not go to school or to a job.
Cognate (Spanish) **vacaciones**

Three Essays

READ To Find Out ▶ What opinions do some students have?

A LONGER, SMARTER VACATION

Each year, our summer **vacation** becomes shorter. I think it should be longer. During summer, students grow and learn.

Some important lessons come from outside of the school walls. One summer, I spent time on a **farm**. I learned how to take care of **crops** and farm animals. It was hard work, but now I understand how important this work is. I think about the farm work when I see all the food in the **supermarket**. This summer, I will **volunteer** at an **animal shelter**. The workers at the shelter will teach me to care for the animals and to help the shelter raise money.

If summer vacation is longer, students will find many different ways to learn.

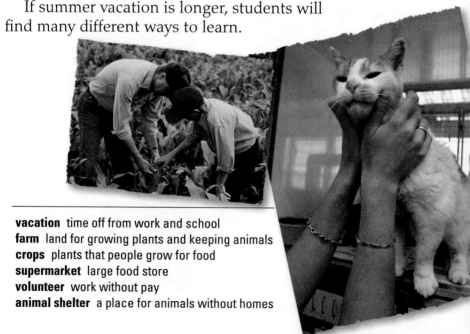

vacation time off from work and school
farm land for growing plants and keeping animals
crops plants that people grow for food
supermarket large food store
volunteer work without pay
animal shelter a place for animals without homes

Ted the Iguana

People are shocked when they see my pet. "What is it?" they ask. He has a face like a frog. His tail is like a snake. Some say that he looks like an **alien** from another **planet**. I tell them that Ted is a giant green iguana. They always have another question. "Why do you want a pet like that?" they ask.

Ted has a fat tongue. He has **spikes** on his head and back. He has sharp nails. Ted is not an ordinary lizard. Ted is gentle. He sits by my feet while I study. It doesn't matter what he looks like. He looks like a member of the family to me. That's why I want a pet like Ted!

alien strange creature
planet object that moves around the sun
spikes long, pointed objects

Hurray for Artists!

I use my imagination to draw. I enjoy **painting** pictures. I can't imagine a school without art class.

Some people don't understand why schools need to teach art, but I do. Students learn about colors. They learn how to draw with crayons, **charcoals**, and other tools. They learn how to pay attention to details.

One year, I entered an art contest. Students worked in **teams**. Together, each team created an art piece. I felt good sharing my ideas about art. The painting showed students like us—different kids who have dreams of doing something important in the future.

Our team was one of the winners of the contest! Now our painting is on a school wall. When I see it, I feel **confident** that I can reach my goals!

painting creating a picture with paints
charcoals black pencils that artists use
teams groups of people that work together
confident sure

What Do You Think? Imagine you wrote an essay for this book. What would you write about? Talk about it with a partner. Make a list of your ideas and share it with the class.

The Best of Both Worlds

Talk About It!

What can our differences teach us?

READ
- Judith Ortiz Cofer: Author in Two Worlds

Prepare To Read

Literary Element
Author's Perspective

Author's perspective is how the author
sees the world. Sometimes authors will tell
the story from a child's perspective. Or, authors
may tell the story from an adult's perspective.
To find an author's perspective

> think about what you know about the author.

> think about the topic.

> look for words that tell you how the author feels about the topic.

Reading Skill Analyze Cultural Context

Every culture has its own customs, or ways of doing things. When
you **analyze cultural context**, you think about the customs and
beliefs of people in a certain place and time. Analyzing cultural
context helps you understand the way characters act. In a
biography, cultural context helps you understand the subject's
perspective. In an autobiography, cultural context helps you
understand the author's perspective.

As you read, complete the graphic organizer in the *Expressions
Practice Book*.

Detail	What It Reveals

Vocabulary for Judith Ortiz Cofer:

Author in Two Worlds   Read the words and definitions below.

accent (ak ' sent) *n.* When a person speaks, you can sometimes hear an **accent** that tells you where the person comes from. Cognate (Spanish) **acento**

conflict (kän' flikt) *n.* A **conflict** is a strong disagreement.
Cognate (Spanish) **conflicto**

island ('ī-lənd) *n.* An area of land surrounded on all sides by water is an **island**. Cognate (Spanish) **isla**

opportunities (ä pər tü ' nə tēz) *n.* When people have chances to succeed, thay have **opportunities**.

peaceful (pēs' fəl) *adj.* Being calm and quiet is to be **peaceful**.

prejudice (pre' jə dəs) *n.* People show **prejudice** when they treat someone in an unkind or unfair way because that someone is different in some way.
Cognate (Spanish) **prejuicio**

rundown (rən' daủn) *adj.* Something that is not in good condition is **rundown**.

traditions (trə di' shən) *n.* **Traditions** are beliefs, stories, and ways of doing things that children learn from their family. Cognate (Spanish) **tradiciones**

Judith Ortiz Cofer: Author in Two Worlds

READ To Find Out — What are important experiences in Judith Ortiz Cofer's life?

The world of Paterson, New Jersey, is much different from the world of Hormigueros, a small town in Puerto Rico. The sun, trees, weather, and even the color of the sky are all very different. Most importantly, the cultures are different. Yet both are part of the culture of the United States.

Judith Ortiz Cofer is a writer who has lived in both cultures. Often, she writes about her experiences living in two cultures. In her poetry and books, she shows what it is like to be both an American, and part of another culture. She writes about the Puerto Rican experience in America, but she speaks for anyone who tries to be a part of American society and does not want to lose his or her home culture.

Judith Cofer was born in Puerto Rico in 1952. Her young parents had different ideas about how their children could succeed in the world. Her mother loved Puerto Rico. The **island** was very important to her, and she felt lost when she was away from it. She held on to the **traditions** and family values of Puerto Rico.

Judith's father was in the United States Navy. He also loved Puerto Rico, but he believed that he did not have many **opportunities** there. He wanted his children to have a good education. He hoped they would have many choices when they grew up. So, when the Navy sent him to Brooklyn, New York, he was happy to go.

---

island land surrounded by water
traditions cultural beliefs, and ways of doing things
opportunities chances

As Judith grew up, this **conflict** of ideas became part of her. When she listened to her mother, she could understand her mother's love of Puerto Rican culture. When her father spoke, she could understand his hope to be part of American culture and have more opportunities. So, when Judith decided to write, these strong ideas showed in her stories, poems, and other writing.

Judith has always lived in two worlds. She left Puerto Rico and began to live in the United States. Yet she did not leave her Puerto Rican culture behind. Although she spent most of her school years in New Jersey, Judith also went to school in Puerto Rico.

"I moved back and forth between cultures," Judith says. As a child, she went from New Jersey to her grandmother's home on the island of Puerto Rico. In her writing, she describes both the **peaceful** life of the island and the more difficult life in Paterson.

conflict strong disagreement
peaceful quiet

LET'S TALK! Describe how Judith's family felt about Puerto Rico and the United States.

READ
To Find Out

What problem did
Judith face?

Like many newcomers in the United States, Judith spoke Spanish at home. She spoke English at school—and everywhere else outside her home. Friends who spoke both languages **teased** her about her **accent**. Judith says she spoke with a Spanish accent when she spoke English. Then she spoke with an English accent when she spoke Spanish. She said that everyone made fun of her "two-way accent."

Judith thought about the problems she had with language when she was a child. She realized that many people who lived in two different worlds would have this problem.

So, Judith used this experience in her writing. Judith writes in English and uses some Spanish words in her writing too. She feels that her style of using both languages at once helps her to reach readers of both cultures. She also can show her own experiences in two cultures better when she adds Spanish words.

---

teased made fun of
accent a way of speaking

What is life like when you move back and forth between two cultures? For Judith, life was full of different sights, different sounds, and different people. In Paterson, New Jersey, Judith lived in "El Building" with other Latino families. It was old and **rundown**. But whenever her father had a long **leave** from the Navy, the family returned to the sunny, warm island. They stayed in her grandmother's home. Judith says she learned the art of telling stories from her grandmother.

"When my **abuela** sat us down to tell a story, we learned something from the story, even though we always laughed," she says. "That was her way of teaching."

Judith learned well. She is not only a writer but also a teacher who shares her stories with both her students and her daughter.

---

rundown not in good condition
leave a break or vacation
abuela grandma

LET'S TALK! What was an important part of Judith's life when she went to Puerto Rico?

READ
To Find Out

What are Judith's accomplishments?

Judith's family moved to Augusta, Georgia when she was 15. She finished her last two years of high school there. As her father had hoped, Judith had choices in the United States. She wanted to have more education, so she took the opportunity to go to college. After she graduated, she began to teach at the University of Georgia in Athens, where she is a professor today.

While she was studying for a **master's degree**, Judith began to write. She says she did not think of becoming a writer when she was a child. As she was studying, she would write quick poems or stories. She felt that she "needed to write." A friend suggested that she send a poem to a **publisher**. When the publisher accepted that one poem, she knew what her life's work would be. She would become a writer.

---

master's degree more education after a college degree
publisher company that makes books

Judith continued to write after she married, using the name Judith Ortiz Cofer. The characters in many of her books are of young people from Puerto Rico who try to honor the culture of their parents. At the same time, they come to change and be part of the culture in other parts of the United States. Often they face **prejudice** from people of both cultures.

"I try to find common ground between people. If you cannot find the **connection** between people, you can never have discussions about anything," she says. With her many experiences in two cultures, Judith Ortiz Cofer has many more stories to tell that will help people understand their differences.

---

prejudice unfair opinions
connection a way to relate or special bond

> **What Do You Think?** Imagine that you are a writer, a painter, or a musician. Which experiences would you want to show in your work? Talk about it with a partner and write your ideas in a web.

Skills and Talent

Talk About It!

Which skills and talents are important to you?

READ • "Campfire"

Literary Element | Form

When you read a poem, you see that it is made up of lines, not sentences. Sometimes, lines are grouped together. These groups of lines are stanzas.

Poetry has different **forms**. Poems that have a **closed form** follow certain rules. Poems with an **open form** have no rules. These poems are called **free verse**.

To identify a free verse poem:

> Think about the rhyme or meter. Free verse can have any type of rhyme or meter.

> Look at the line length and stanzas. Free verse can have any kind of line length or stanza.

Practice Read the poem. With a partner, explain why this is a free verse poem.

> The night sky is bright with stars
> and dark planets.
> Somewhere Mercury and Venus burn hot.
> Far away Pluto freezes.
> Here is Earth
> A human home.

As you read, complete the graphic organizer in the *Expressions Practice Book*.

Length of Lines	End Rhyme	What Kind of Poem is This?

Vocabulary for "Campfire"

Read the words and definitions below.

age (āj') *n.* You tell your **age** when you tell how old you are.

catch (kach') *v.* To **catch** something, you must chase it or try to get it in some way.

luscious (lə' shəs) *adj.* When something tastes **luscious**, it is very good to eat.

roast (rōst') *v.* You **roast** food when you cook it over a fire.

rustling (rə' səl ing) *adj.* You are **rustling** when you move your hands around in things and make a soft noise.

sparks (spärks') *n.* **Sparks** are tiny bits of fire that fly into the air. Sparks are bright.

tent (tent') *n.* Some people sleep in a **tent** when they go camping.

woods (wudz') *n.* If you go to the **woods**, you go to an area with many trees.

Campfire

by Janet S. Wong

Just think—
when Mother was my **age**,
she could build a fire
with **sparks** from rocks,
catch a bunch of
grasshoppers and
roast them whole
for a summer
night's snack!

---

age number of years since birth
sparks small burning particles in the air
catch capture

roast cook over an open fire

"Get me a good stick,"
she says, "thin but strong."
and I bring her one
from the **woods**
behind our **tent**.
On the way back
I see a brown bag
by her feet—
could it be?

When the fire is spitting ready,
she reaches
in the bag, **rustling**,
and hands me
one big, fat, **luscious**
marshmallow.

---

woods many trees in an area
tent shelter used when camping
rustling sound of one's hand moving around
in a bag
luscious very good to eat

What Do You Think? Think of someone else who has
been the first to do something. Who was the person and what
did he or she do first? Why was it important? Talk in small
groups and use the sentence frames below.

___was the first person to _____. It was important
because___.

Famous FIRSTS
in Women's History

READ • The First First Ladies

Talk About It!

When might you choose
to put others first?

249

Prepare To Read

Literary Element Text Features

Text features are the pictures, charts, maps, and other **graphics** in a text. They show information that helps you understand the text better. When you read

❯ look at the drawings, maps, graphs, and other features on each page.

❯ think about how these features help you understand the text.

Practice Look at the map. What information is on this map? Talk about the information with a partner.

The United States of America

Reading Strategy Summarize

When you **summarize**, you retell what happened in a few words. Summaries tell only the main ideas and important details in a text. To summarize a text

❯ think about questions that answer *Who?*, *What?*, *When?*, *Where?*, *Why?*, and *How?*

❯ include only the main ideas and important details.

❯ retell it using your own words.

As you read, complete the graphic organizer in the *Expressions Practice Book*.

First Lady	Event	Why It Is Important
Martha Washington		
Abigail Adams		
Dolley Madison		

Vocabulary for The First First Ladies

Read the words and definitions below.

active (ak′ tiv) *adj.* When you are **active**, you are doing things.
Cognate (Spanish) **activo(a)**

debating (di bāt′ ing) *v.* When you are **debating**, you are using facts and opinions to talk with others about an idea.
Cognate (Spanish) **debatir**

example (ig zam′ pəl) *n.* A model of how to do something is an **example**.
Cognate (Spanish) **ejemplo**

household (haus′ hōld) *n.* A **household** is a family and all the other people who live in a home.

independence (in də pen′ dəns) *n.* When you do not rely on anyone else, you have **independence**.
Cognate (Spanish) **independencia**

injured (in′jərd) *adj.* When your body gets hurt, you are **injured**.

organized (or′ gə nīzd) *v.* When you have planned all the details of an event, you have **organized** it.
Cognate (Spanish) **organizar**

serious (sir′ē əs) *adj.* a **serious** person is one who is thoughtful and grave.

The First First Ladies

READ To Find Out — What special role did Martha Washington have?

The wife of the president of the United States is the First Lady.

The paintings of early First Ladies don't tell us much. They show older women who look **serious**. They have their hands folded on their laps. But the real First Ladies were more **active** than they appear in their paintings. They each helped shape our young nation in their own way.

Martha Washington

When George Washington became the first president of the United States, Martha became the First Lady. The people of the United States felt the president and First Lady should not lead as a king or queen would. They should set a different **example**.

---

serious thoughtful and grave
active busy working and doing many things
example a model for what someone else does

252

Martha Washington had already done much to help her husband be a great leader. George Washington was in charge of the army when the U.S. fought for **independence** from England. Martha ran the family farms and large **household** while her husband was at war. She also **organized** her **servants** to make cloth for uniforms and **bandages** for soldiers. They knitted warm scarves, stockings, and sweaters.

independence freedom
household a group or family living together
organized planned all the details
servants those who work for a household
bandages strips of cloth used to cover cuts or other wounds

They also prepared fresh meals. Martha took these **supplies** to the soldiers herself. She sent **nurses** to help those who were **injured**.

When George Washington became America's first president, his wife was proud **to serve** as First Lady. She welcomed many visitors to the presidential home in New York. She helped show the world that although America was a young nation, it was a proud nation.

LET'S TALK! Why did Martha Washington have to be an example?

supplies necessary food and equipment
nurses people trained to help sick or wounded people
injured hurt
to serve to do a duty

254

READ
To Find Out

Why was Abigail Adams different from most women of her time?

Abigail Adams

John Adams was vice president when George Washington was president. Then, John Adams became the second president. His wife Abigail Adams became the second First Lady. Abigail Adams loved this challenge and was not afraid to say what she thought.

As a child, Abigail taught herself how to read. She also learned all she could from her grandfather about politics. Unlike most women, Abigail Adams loved **debating** politics. She enjoyed talking about politics with her husband John Adams. When he traveled, Abigail sent him letters filled with her news and opinions. She **argued** against **slavery**, even though many people had slaves. She argued that women should be able to vote. John Adams often shared his wife's letters with other politicians. He often asked Abigail to help him with his **speeches**. In this way, Abigail Adams helped to guide the politics of her day.

debating discussing facts and opinions with others
argued spoke out for an idea
slavery the practice of owning people to do hard work
speeches public talks

255

Dolley Madison

Dolley Madison became the third First Lady when her husband James Madison was **elected** president in 1809. President Madison was a serious man. His wife was much more **social**. She enjoyed welcoming people to the White House and entertaining them.

LET'S TALK! Who was Dolley Madison?

elected chosen by voters
social enjoys being with others

256

Yet this First Lady could be serious as well. In 1812, the United States and England were at war. Late one night, British troops were marching toward Washington, D. C. President Madison was away, having gone to visit the **army**. The First Lady was alone at the White House with her servants.

army a group of soldiers

257

Dolley Madison stayed calm. She packed up the **original** copies of the Constitution and the Declaration of Independence. She also packed up a famous painting of George Washington. Her servants put these items on a wagon to be taken to **safety**. The First Lady left shortly before British soldiers reached the White House. The soldiers burned it down, leaving only the stone walls. Thanks to the brave First Lady, all was not lost.

Martha Washington, Abigail Adams, and Dolley Madison lived and served long ago. Still, they are remembered today as women who helped define the role of the First Lady.

---

original the first or only of its kind
safety free from harm

What Do You Think? Think of someone else who has been the first to do something. Who was the person and what did he or she do first? Why was it important? Talk with a partner and use the sentence frames below.

___ was the first person to ___. It was important because ___.

Time for a Change

Talk About It!

Why should all people have the same rights?

READ • Women and the Right to Vote

Prepare To Read

Literary Element Text Features

Text features are the graphics in a text. Graphics include photos, charts, and timelines. A **timeline** shows events in the order they happened. Timelines can have dates, labels, and pictures.

Practice Read the timeline. What information is in the timeline? Talk about it with a partner.

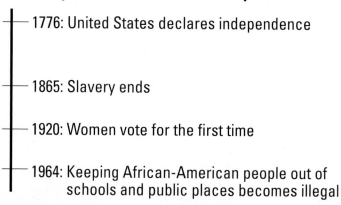

Important Dates in U. S. History

— 1776: United States declares independence

— 1865: Slavery ends

— 1920: Women vote for the first time

— 1964: Keeping African-American people out of schools and public places becomes illegal

Reading Strategy Summarize

When you **summarize**, you retell a text in your own words. A good summary includes main ideas and important details. Summarizing helps you make sure that you understand what you have read.

As you read, complete the graphic organizer in the *Expressions Practice Book*.

Event	When It Happened	Why It Is Important

Vocabulary for Women and the Right to Vote

Read the words and definitions below.

ballot (ba' lət) *n.* A **ballot** is a sheet of paper for marking your vote.
Cognate (Spanish) **balota**

elect (i lekt') *v.* When you choose someone for a political office, you **elect** him or her.
Cognate (Spanish) **elegir**

equality (i kwä' lə tē) *n.* People who want **equality** think everyone should have the same opportunities and rights.

picket (pi' kət) *v.* When you **picket**, you stand outside a store or business and try to convince other people not to go in.

radical (ra' di kəl) *adj.* Something that is extreme and different is **radical**.
Cognate (Spanish) **radical**

vote (vōt') *v.* To make a choice by ballot or show of hands is to **vote**.
Cognate (Spanish) **votar**

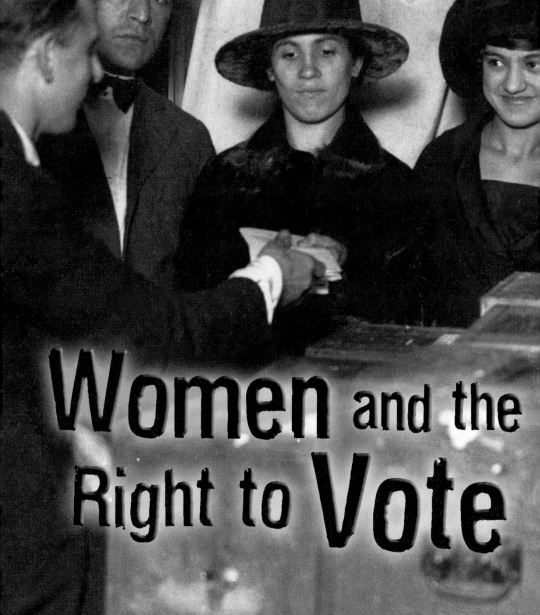

Women and the Right to Vote

Today, women in this country **vote** just as men do. For much of our nation's history though, only men could vote. Women had to fight for this right.

When the United States was a young country, men did not believe women should be able to vote. Abigail Adams felt this was unfair. Abigail Adams wanted **equality** for women. Her husband John Adams worked for the new government. John Adams and other leaders were creating laws for the new nation. Abigail Adams wrote letters pushing her husband to act for equality. "Remember the Ladies," Abigail Adams wrote. Yet, her ideas were too new. The new **Constitution** did not allow women to vote.

vote to make a choice by ballot or show of hands
equality the same opportunities for everyone
Constitution document that explains a nation's laws and ideas

263

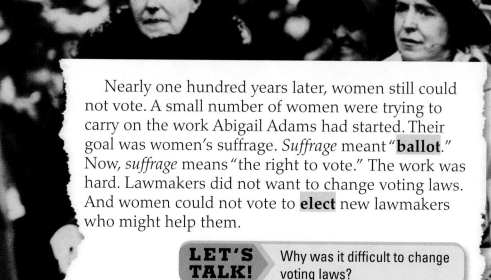

Nearly one hundred years later, women still could not vote. A small number of women were trying to carry on the work Abigail Adams had started. Their goal was women's suffrage. *Suffrage* meant "**ballot**." Now, *suffrage* means "the right to vote." The work was hard. Lawmakers did not want to change voting laws. And women could not vote to **elect** new lawmakers who might help them.

LET'S TALK! Why was it difficult to change voting laws?

ballot paper used to state a secret decision
elect to choose a leader

Women's Suffrage

Study the timeline.
How many years passed between Abigail Adams writing "Remember the Ladies" and women winning the right to vote?

1776: ▲
Abigail Adams writes "Remember the Ladies."

1848: ▲
Susan B. Anthony sets goals for women's rights.

1872: ▲
Police arrest Susan B. Anthony when she tries to vote for president.

1890: ▲
The National American Woman Suffrage Association is formed.

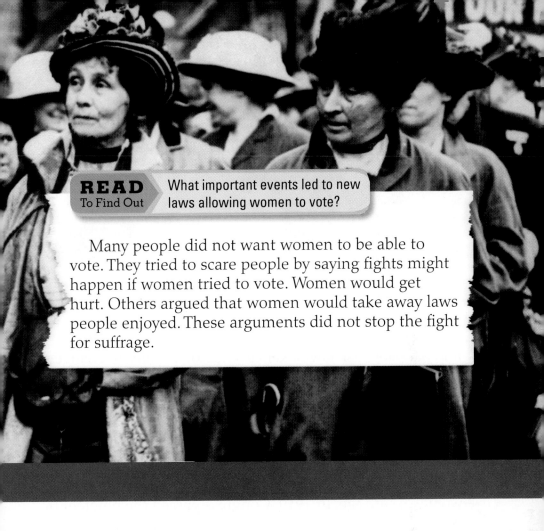

READ
To Find Out

What important events led to new laws allowing women to vote?

Many people did not want women to be able to vote. They tried to scare people by saying fights might happen if women tried to vote. Women would get hurt. Others argued that women would take away laws people enjoyed. These arguments did not stop the fight for suffrage.

1913: ▲
The Congressional **Union** is formed.

1916: ▲
Jeannette Rankin of Montana becomes the first American woman elected to **Congress.**

1917: ▲
President Wilson supports women's suffrage.

1920: ▲
Women win the right to vote.

Union a group of people joined for a common purpose
Congress a group of people elected to make laws

Susan B. Anthony did something **radical** to get people's attention. In 1872, Anthony walked into a voting **booth** where she tried to vote for President Ulysses S. Grant. The police arrested her. Julia Ward Howe was less radical. She told people to ask lawmakers in their own states to change voting laws. Finally, the Wyoming Territory allowed women to vote before it became a state. Other states followed. In 1913, Alice Paul asked people to **picket** at the White House to show their support for women's suffrage. Thousands of people went to the White House to picket.

In 1917, President Woodrow Wilson decided to support women's suffrage. In 1919, Congress passed the nineteenth **Amendment**. The following year, women finally won the right to vote.

---

radical extreme
booth a small, private room
picket stopping others from entering a building
Amendment change to the Constitution

What Do You Think? Look back at the timeline. What do you think are the most important events in the women's suffrage movement? With a partner, choose two events and discuss why you think they are the most important.

Caring About Earth

Talk About It!

Why should you care
about Earth?

READ
- "The Once that Never Was"
- Resources—Now and in the Future

267

Prepare To Read

Literary Element Allusion

An **allusion** connects readers to something outside of the text. Allusions help readers compare the text with something familiar. An allusion can connect to

> a character from another book or a movie.

> people or events from history.

> actors, writers, and musicians.

> songs and art.

Reading Strategy Draw Conclusions About Author's Perspective

Author's perspective is the author's feelings about a subject. Sometimes authors state their feelings directly. When you **draw conclusions about the author's perspective**, you have to decide what the author's feelings are. As you read a text, think about

> the main idea.

> the words the author uses.

> the author's purpose for writing.

> the author's audience.

As you read, complete the graphic organizer in the *Expressions Practice Book*.

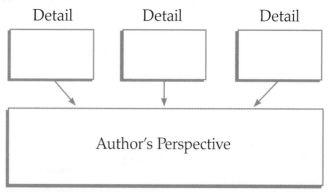

Read the words and definitions below.

coasts (kōsts') *n.* The areas of land next to the sea are the **coasts**. Cognate (Spanish) **costas**

polar bear (pō' lər ber') *n.* A large animal with white fur is a **polar bear**. It lives in cold, icy regions.

hunting (hən' ting) *v.* When you are looking for something, you are **hunting** for it.

town (taun') *n.* A small city is a **town**.

lucky (lə' kē) *adj.* When something good happens and you do not expect it, you feel **lucky**.

wise (wīz') *adj.* If you are **wise**, you are smart and make good decisions.

The Once that Never Was

by Barbara Giles

READ To Find Out — What characters and things do you already know?

The Once that Never Was may be
sooner than dreamed of. Suddenly
we'll find ourselves about to land
on **coasts** of fabled Samarkand.
There Doctor Who, quite settled down,
will show us all the sights of **town**
and Lancelot and Guinevere
will take us **hunting polar bear**.

---

coasts lands at the edges of oceans
town small city
hunting looking for
polar bear large white animal that lives in the snow

Luke Skywalker will tell his story
of star wars and **galactic** glory,
and Eve shall pick us apples which
make people happy, **lucky**, rich.
There Sleeping Beauty, wide awake,
lives in her castle by the lake.
The towers of Troy, all sunlit, rise
and simple Simon has grown **wise**.
For everything that ever was
is found in Once that Never Was,
all things pleasant, all things good.

What is that **roaring** in the wood?

---

galactic in outer space
lucky having good things happen
wise smart
roaring sound of an angry animal

What Do You Think? In a small group, list all of the characters in the poem. Next to each, write what the poem says about each character. Then write what you know about the character. Talk about how your ideas are different from what the poem says.

Vocabulary for Resources—

Now and in the Future   Read the words and definitions below.

engines (en' jənz) *n.* **Engines** are machines that make things work.

pollution (pə lü' shən) *n.* **Pollution** is the dirt and garbage in the air, water, and land.

natural resource (na' chə rəl rē' sor sez) *n.* Something from Earth that humans can use is a **natural resource**.

Cognate (Spanish) **recurso natural**

recycle (rē sī' kəl) *v.* When you use something again you **recycle**.

Cognate (Spanish) **reciclar**

non-renewable resources (nän' rē nü'ə bəl rē' sor sez) *n.* You cannot replace **non-renewable resources**.

Cognate (Spanish) **recursos no renovables**

vehicles (ve' ə kəlz) *n.* People ride or carry things in **vehicles**.

Cognate (Spanish) **vehículos**

Resources—
Now and in the Future

READ
To Find Out

What are some
natural resources?

Everything that comes from nature is a **natural resource**. Sunlight that warms us is a natural resource. Soil used to grow plants is a natural resource too. So is the air we breathe. You depend on Earth's resources to live. Think about the many ways you use water each day. You use water to cook, brush your teeth, go swimming, and wash. Most important, your body needs water to live.

Water, air, and even trees are **renewable resources**. They can be replaced. People cut down trees to build houses. Yet people can plant new trees to replace the ones they use. Other kinds of natural resources are **non-renewable resources**. They cannot be replaced. For example, we use oil, coal, and gas to power machines and heat our homes. We cannot make more of these resources after we use them. They come from deep in the Earth and formed over **thousands** of years. We call them **fossil fuels**.

---

natural resource something from the Earth that people use
renewable resources things that you can replace
non-renewable resources things that you can use only once
thousands very many; hundreds and hundreds
fossil fuels energy sources that formed over
thousands of years

Fossil Fuels and Pollution

When people use fossil fuels, they often cause **pollution**. Pollution is harmful to our land, air, and water. For example, ships must carry oil across the ocean for use in other places. These ships may have accidents and spill their oil into the water. The thick, sticky oil kills the ocean plants and animals. It then can wash up onto beaches. The oil is very hard to clean off rocks and soil. Some is always left behind.

Fossil fuels are burned to make energy. At the same time, they release **gases** that pollute the air. Air pollution can be dangerous for people and Earth. It can cause breathing problems for people, and it can kill plants and animals. Scientists even worry that air pollution is causing Earth's temperature to rise. They do not know how this might affect life on Earth.

LET'S TALK! How can fossil fuels harm people and Earth?

pollution dirt in the air, water, and land
gases like air, a substance that has no shape or size of its own

READ
To Find Out

How does the way we live affect the health of Earth?

Fuel and How we Live

Do you ride in a car or bus to get to school each day? People use **gasoline** to power their cars or other **vehicles**. Many cars cause pollution when their **engines** burn gas.

The average vehicle can travel 18 miles on one gallon of gas. In California, drivers travel about 36 miles each day. How many gallons would an average vehicle need per day? Yes, every driver uses two gallons of gas each day.

In California, people use about 24 million vehicles. If these vehicles could travel 30 miles on one gallon of gas, people could save about 500 million gallons of gasoline each month. They would be saving a non-renewable resource, and the air would be cleaner.

---

gasoline a liquid fossil fuel, also called "gas"
vehicles cars, trucks, or other types of transportation
engines machines that make things move

Small Actions Make a Difference

People can take small steps to **conserve** Earth's resources. Here are some ideas:

- Turn off the water when brushing teeth.
- Share a ride with others.
- Ride a bike to school.
- Take a bus or train.
- Turn off lights and the TV when not in use.
- Use less of something. Save paper and plastic bags to use again. Find new uses for old things.
- **Recycle** cans, glass, paper, metal, and plastic.

Think about what you and your family can do to help Earth—for now and for the future.

---

conserve save
recycle to use something again

What Do You Think? Talk with a partner about different ways you use natural resources and what you can do to conserve them. Use the sentence frame below.

Every day I use natural resources to _____.
I can conserve them by_____.

Writing Workshop

Writing That Teaches
What brings out the best in you? Think about the challenges that have made you the person you are today. Many important figures have also experienced challenges and used their inner strengths to do great things.

Writing Assignment
For this Writing Workshop, you will find information on and write a **research report** about a historical figure and the events in that figure's life. Write your research report for your classmates and your teacher. They will be your audience.

WRITING PLAN

> Choose an interesting person to be the subject of your research report.

> Use multiple sources to find information that you know is true.

> Use facts that you find during your research to support the main idea of the report.

> Include a list of sources, or bibliography, and **footnotes**.

Writing Model
Read the student model below.

Gandhi was a man who lived in India. He went to college and studied to be a lawyer. After college, he worked in South Africa as a lawyer. He was treated very badly there. When he spoke out about the unfair treatment, he was beaten and put in jail. But he did not stop speaking out. He kept working to help the poor and mistreated have peace and equality.

Prewrite

1. **Gather Ideas**
   To get started on your research report, think about interesting people you have studied. Talk with friends and family about famous people. Read Internet sites and library books about famous people. Make a list of the names of people who interest you.

2. **Choose a Topic**
   Review your list. Choose the person you find most interesting or admire most. Then you will have to do research to find out more about the figure you chose. As you search for information sources, record the following information for each source:
   - Name of source
   - Author
   - Page number or Internet address
   - Publication information

3. **Get Organized**
   Review your notes and organize your ideas into an **outline**. In the outline, first state what the figure has done to affect history. Below that, state the important events and actions in the figure's life that support your statement.

   Gandhi dedicated his life to helping Indians gain peace and equality.
   I. Gandhi experienced racism personally.
      A. He was treated badly in South Africa.
      B. He wanted Indians to gain freedom from Great Britain.
   II. Gandhi taught that peace brings change.
      A. Gandhi led Indians to protest the British tax on salt.
      B. Gandhi did not believe in violence.

Draft

1. **Start Writing**
   Use your outline to help you write your research report.

2. **Add to Your Draft**
   Support your statements with facts from your sources. Put the name of the author and the page number in **parentheses** at the end of the sentence.

   > In 1932, Gandhi went on a hunger strike. Because of this, he became very famous throughout the world (Severance 66).

   End with a **summary**.

   > Gandhi inspired an entire nation to use peace to bring change. Even today people try to follow Gandhi's model of peace and forgiveness.

   Include sources on the **bibliography** or **works cited** page.

   > Severance, John C. Gandhi: Great Soul. New York: Clarion, 1997.

USE GOOD WRITING TRAITS: SENTENCE FLUENCY
Sentence fluency is a smooth flow from sentence to sentence or from paragraph to paragraph. **Transition words** like *then*, *however*, and *later* make sentences flow better. These **words** act as links from one sentence to another.

Read the example below. Which word or words help link ideas and create sentence fluency?

> Gandhi was sad about his mother's death, but he had to take care of his family. So he stayed strong and kept working hard.

Revise

Now it's time to revise your draft. This step helps you make your writing better, so that others will want to read it.

1. **Read Your Research Report** Ask yourself these questions:
   - Does the report present a real figure from history?
   - Does the report present facts about the figure's life?
   - Is there a bibliography or works cited page at the end?

2. **Show Your Research Report** Trade drafts with a partner. Answer these questions as you read your partner's research report.
   - Can you tell who the report is about?
   - Are the main points supported by facts that are true?
   - Are the supporting facts presented in an order that makes sense?
   - Does the report use multiple sources of information?

3. **Make Your Changes** Talk with your partner to help you decide what changes you need to make. Then revise your draft.

Technology You can use the Internet to find many sources of information. But it is important to only use sources you can trust. Try to use only sites that end in .org, .edu, or .gov in your research. When you are ready to write, use the design features in your word processing software to add graphics, such as a timeline or photo, to your report.

Edit and Proofread

1. **Proofread Your Report** Reread your research report. Look for mistakes in capitalization, punctuation, or spelling. Use the proofreading symbols in the chart on page 353 to mark changes.

2. **Check Your Sentences** Did you use complete sentences? Do subjects and verbs agree? Make changes if you need to.

Grammar Focus: Commas in Dates and Place Names

When you write about a person's life, be careful about how you present dates and places.

Problem: Unfamiliar locations can be confusing.

> Gandhi's father was prime minister of Porbandar India.

Solution: Separate cities, states, and countries with commas.

> Gandhi's father was prime minister of Porbandar, India.

Problem: Commas are missing from the bibliography entry.

> Severance John C. Gandhi: Great Soul. New York: Clarion 1997.

Solution: Use a comma to separate the first and last name of the author. Place a comma between the publisher and the date of publication.

> Severance, John C. Gandhi: Great Soul. New York: Clarion, 1997.

3. **Make a Final Copy** Make the corrections that you marked. If you are working on the computer, print out the corrected work. If not, rewrite it.

Present

Here are some ways to share your writing.

- Give your research report to your friends to read and ask them for their comments.

- Have a friend read your report and tell you what he or she feels about the figure you selected for the report.

⬛ Speaking, Listening, and Viewing Workshop

Oral Report

Activity

1. **Connect to Your Writing**
   Give an oral report on the life of a historical figure to your classmates. Use the research report you wrote for the Writing Workshop on pages 277–281.

2. **Plan Your Oral Report**
   Reread your research report. Mark the parts that you want to include in your oral report. Remember to give your oral report in the same order that your research report is in. Your oral report should present well-researched information on a focused topic. If possible, use visual aids.

3. **Rehearse Your Oral Report**
   Practice your oral report in front of a mirror. Watch your facial expressions and gestures. Listen to the volume and style of your voice. Practice until you feel ready. Write important points on note cards for you to use during your oral report.

4. **Deliver Your Oral Report**
   - Speak clearly.
   - Change the pace and volume of your speaking. Slow down to explain confusing parts of the topic.
   - Use visual aids to help you explain information in your report.

Listening to Learn

As you listen to another student's oral report, take notes. Did you understand why the figure was so important? Share your ideas with the student. Use the sentence frame below.

- I found this piece of information the most interesting: ___. What is the source of that information?

Friends to the End

Talk About It!

Why is friendship important?

READ
- Damon and Pythias
- Greek Drama

Prepare To Read

Literary Element | Dialogue

Dialogue is a conversation between characters. When characters speak, you learn more about them and their feelings about other characters. As you read, think about what you learn about each character from dialogue.

Practice Read the dialogue from a play. What can you learn about each character? Talk about it with a partner.

> DAD: I want to give you this watch. Grandfather
>   used to wear it.
>
> DANIEL: You can trust me, Dad. I'll take care of it.

Reading Skill | Analyze Diction

Diction is the words an author chooses. Authors choose words carefully to help readers understand the meaning or feeling of the story. When you **analyze diction**, you think about how certain words make the message of the story clear. As you read, complete the graphic organizer in the *Expressions Practice Book*.

Word	Denotation— Dictionary Definition	Connotation— Positive, Negative, or Neutral

Vocabulary for Damon and Pythias

Read the words and definitions below.

crime (krīm′) *n.* A **crime** is an act that breaks a law. Stealing is a crime. Cognate (Spanish) **crimen**

disagree (dis ə grē′) *v.* When you believe something different than someone else, you **disagree**.

prison (pri′ zən) *n.* A **prison** is a place with guards. People who have done something wrong stay there and cannot leave.
Cognate (Spanish) **prisión**

promise (prä′ məs) *v.* When you **promise**, you say something that you will or will not do.
Cognate (Spanish) **promesar**

return (ri tərn′) *v.* To come back again is to **return**.

save (sāv′) *v.* You **save** someone when you protect that person from danger.

trust (trəst′) *v.* You **trust** someone when you believe that the person will not lie.

unfair (ən fer′) *adj.* When a law or rule is **unfair**, some people have more rights than others.

DAMON AND PYTHIAS

Characters

Damon	First Man
Pythias	First Woman
King	Second Man
Narrator	Second Woman
Mother	Robber

READ To Find Out — Why is life hard for people in Sicily?

NARRATOR: A long time ago, two men named Damon and Pythias lived in Sicily. Everyone knew them because they were very good friends—best friends. A **cruel** king ruled Sicily. He made **unfair** laws. Life was very hard for the people. Everyone did what the king wanted. Everyone was afraid to **disagree** with the king. Only two people, Damon and Pythias, were not afraid.

---

cruel mean
unfair not just or right
disagree have different opinions about

SCENE ONE

KING: Pythias! You do not agree with my laws. Is this true?

PYTHIAS: Yes, it is true! Many people disagree with your laws. People are afraid to speak.

KING: Take Pythias to **prison**!

PYTHIAS: Oh, King! What is my **crime**? I told you the truth. I want to make life better for your people. Why do I have to go to prison?

KING: You disagree with me. That is your crime, Pythias. You will stay in prison for two weeks. Then, **guards** will kill you. The people will watch you die.

END SCENE

LET'S TALK! Why is Pythias in prison?

prison a place where people who have done something wrong must stay
crime an action that breaks the law
guards people who watch over the prison

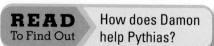
NARRATOR: Soon, everyone in Sicily knew Pythias was in prison. Damon went to see Pythias. Damon was a good friend.

DAMON: Oh, Pythias! This prison is cold. You have no food. It is a terrible place! I wish I could **save** you!

PYTHIAS: No one can save me. My friend, will you please take care of my mother and sister?

DAMON: Yes, I will.

PYTHIAS: Will you **promise**?

DAMON: I promise that I will take care of them. I will give my word. They will be like my family.

PYTHIAS: You are a good friend. I wish I could see my mother and sister before I die. But they live far away. I cannot leave this prison!

DAMON: I will go to the king now. I will ask him to let you visit your family. I will take your place in prison. If you do not **return**, the king can kill me.

PYTHIAS: No, no, Damon! Stop!

END SCENE

SCENE THREE

DAMON: King! Let Pythias visit his mother and sister. I will take his place. I will stay in prison until Pythias returns. You may kill me if he does not return.

KING: You are a **fool**, Damon. Pythias will not return. You will die.

DAMON: I **trust** Pythias with my life.

KING: Then Pythias may go. Take this letter to the prison. You will stay in prison and wait for Pythias to return.

END SCENE

---

save to protect from danger
promise swear to do something
return to come back again
fool a person who is not smart and can be tricked easily
trust to believe in

SCENE FOUR

NARRATOR: Everyone in Sicily talked about Damon and Pythias.

FIRST MAN: Will Pythias come back?

FIRST WOMAN: Ha! I do not believe so. He does not want to die!

SECOND MAN: No, Pythias is a good man. He will not let the king kill Damon.

SECOND WOMAN: Even a good man does not want to die.

FIRST MAN: Yes, Pythias wants to live. But, he wants Damon to live, too. Pythias will come back.

SECOND MAN: Pythias has many days to return. He will return. He and Damon are best friends.

FIRST WOMAN: Friendship is important. But it is not as important as your life. Pythias will not return.

END SCENE

LET'S TALK! What does the first woman believe?

READ
To Find Out

What happens when
Pythias visits his home?

SCENE FIVE

NARRATOR: Damon stayed in prison. Pythias traveled
home to see his mother and his sister. He said good-bye to
his family for the last time.

MOTHER: Pythias, don't leave. I beg you. Stay one more
day!

PYTHIAS: I cannot stay. Damon, my friend, will die if I
don't return. Please, don't cry!

END SCENE

SCENE SIX

NARRATOR: Pythias walked quickly through the forest. He stopped when someone called him.

ROBBER: You, there! Stop!

PYTHIAS: What do you want?

ROBBER: Give me your money!

PYTHIAS: I will give it to you, but please let me go. The king will kill my friend if I do not return.

ROBBER: I will not kill you.

NARRATOR: The robber took the money and tied Pythias to a tree. Then he ran away. It took Pythias a whole day to **untie** himself. He was hungry and thirsty. But he could not stop for food. He traveled all day and night. He hoped he was not too late. He hoped he could save Damon.

END SCENE

LET'S TALK! The robber meets Pythias in the forest. How does this affect Damon?

---

untie to free from being tied

SCENE SEVEN

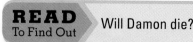

NARRATOR: The guards took Damon to the public square. They tied his hands behind his back. The people started to get angry. They did not want Damon to die. Pythias had less than one hour to save his friend. The king arrived.

FIRST WOMAN: Long live the king!

FIRST MAN: The king is cruel! He is unfair!

KING: Damon, it is almost time for you to die. Pythias has not returned.

DAMON: I do not believe it is his **fault**. Something has stopped him. I **forgive** him. I am happy to die for my friend.

KING: Guard, take this man to the ...

FIRST MAN: Look! Pythias has returned!

SECOND MAN: Pythias promised that he would return! He has returned! I knew it!

PYTHIAS: Damon must not die! Let me through! Damon!

DAMON: Pythias, my friend! I knew you would return!

ALL VOICES: Set them free! Set them free!

KING: My people! I am the king. I have a great army. I am very rich. But I do not have the most important thing. I do not have a good friend like Damon or Pythias. I have been cruel and unfair. Now I could never kill two men who are such good friends. Damon and Pythias, you are free!

END

---

fault responsibility for a mistake or error
forgive to give up or let go of anger against

What Do You Think? Take the part of Damon or Pythias and let your partner take the other part. Imagine you are talking to students today about how to be a good friend. Complete the sentence below.

A good friend should ___.

293

Vocabulary for Greek Drama

Read the words and definitions below.

amphitheatres (am' fə thē tərs) *n.* **Amphitheatres** are outdoor theatres that ancient Greeks used for plays.

Cognate (Spanish) **anfiteatro**

morals (mor' əlz) *n.* **Morals** are beliefs about what is right and wrong.

Cognate (Spanish) **moralejas**

costumes (käs' tümz) *n.* The clothing, jewelry, and make-up that actors wear in a play are part of the **costumes**.

perform (pə fórm') *v.* When you act in front of others, you **perform**.

drama (drä' mə) *n.* A **drama** is a story or play. Actors tell the story on a stage.

pretend (pri tend') *v.* When you **pretend**, you act a part to tell a story.

festivals (fes' tə vəl) *n.* **Festivals** are celebrations to remember an event.

scenery (sē'nə rē) *n.* The walls and painting behind the actors on a stage are the **scenery**.

GREEK DRAMA

READ To Find Out — What kinds of plays did ancient Greeks enjoy?

Have you ever wanted to be the star in a **drama**? A drama is a story that is a play. Actors who **pretend** to be different characters tell the story. You might watch a drama on television or at the movie theater. You might go to a play to see a drama, just as the **ancient** Greeks did.

Drama began in Greece more than 2,000 years ago. The plays were part of religious **festivals**. The two main kinds of drama were the **tragedy** and the **comedy**. In a tragedy, something bad happens. The ending of the play is not happy. A comedy is drama with a happy ending.

drama a play or story that is acted on a stage
pretend take the role of; act like
ancient a long time ago
festivals celebrations
tragedy very sad set of events
comedy very funny set of events

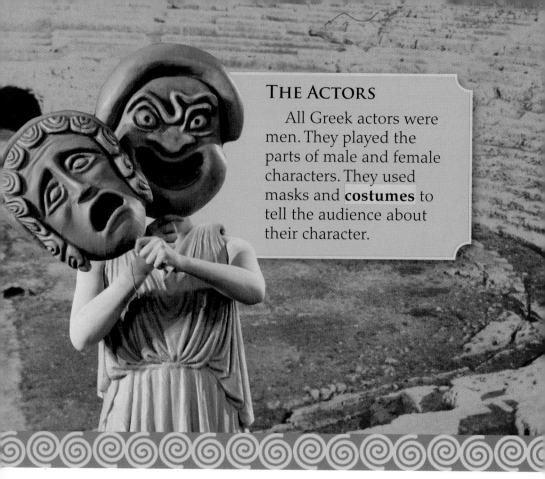

The people who watched the dramas wanted to enjoy the story. They also wanted to learn new ideas about religion and **morals**. After they watched the dramas, the people would talk about the new ideas and decide if they agreed with them or not.

FAMOUS WRITERS

Some famous drama writers of ancient Greece were Aeschylus (EHS•kuh•luhs), Sophocles, (SAH•fuh•KLEEZ) and Euripides (yu•RIH•puh•DEEZ). These **playwrights** wrote tragedies. Aristophanes (AIR•ih•STOH•fuh•NEEZ) wrote comedies. Today, actors still **perform** their dramas on the stage.

---

costumes masks and clothing that actors wear on a stage
morals beliefs about what is good and bad
playwrights people who write dramas or plays
perform act out before an audience

Aeschylus wrote plays for two actors. The actors wore costumes and carried objects that showed something about their character. Aeschylus wrote *Oresteia* (ohr•eh•STY•uh). This drama is a tragedy. It is the story of a king who returns from a war with Troy.

Sophocles wrote dramas for three actors instead of two. His plays had **scenery** behind the actors. His play *Antigone* (an•TIH•guh•nee) is about a difficult problem. The characters have to decide if it is better to follow orders or do what is right.

---

scenery walls and pictures on a stage that show the setting

OUTDOOR THEATERS

In ancient Greece, people sat in outdoor theaters to watch plays. In these **amphitheatres**, the seats were on a hillside. The stage was the open space at the bottom of the hill. Today, some communities have outdoor theaters like those in ancient Greece.

Euripides wrote plays about everyday Greek life. He wanted people to think about ideas, too. The ideas might be about war, how to raise children, or what a government should do.

Aristophanes wrote comedies that made fun of important people. In his plays, actors told jokes that made people laugh and think about new ideas, also.

---

amphitheatres outdoor theaters

What Do You Think? Compare the way people in ancient Greece went to see dramas with how and what you watch today. What is the same? What is different? Talk about it with a partner. Make a list of your ideas.

LESSON 28

Living Your Dreams

Talk About It!

What are your goals?

READ • Felipe's Photos

Prepare To Read

Literary Element Stage Directions

Stage directions are a playwright's instructions to the actors, the director, and the stage crew. Stage directions are the words in a script that appear in italicized type within parentheses. The actors do not read stage directions aloud. They read the stage directions silently so they know what to do or how to say their lines.

Stage directions give you extra information about a play. They help you imagine how a play looks and sounds when actors perform it.

Reading Skill Identify Cause-and-Effect Relationships

Cause and effect describes a relationship between events in a story. A **cause** is person or event that makes something happen. An **effect** is what happens. Read the following example:

Cause: You practice the piano every day.
Effect: You play the piano well.

To identify cause-and-effect relationships, ask yourself these questions:
• What happened?
• Why did it happen?

As you read, complete the graphic organizer in the *Expressions Practice Book*.

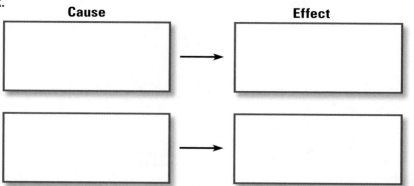

Read the words and definitions below.

career (kə rēr') *n.* The job or work you plan to do during your life is your **career**.

Cognate (Spanish) **carrera**

secret (sē' krət) *n.* A **secret** is information you keep from others.

Cognate (Spanish) **secreto**

convince (kən vins') *v.* You **convince** someone when you make the person believe what you think or say.

Cognate (Spanish) **convencer**

stubborn (stə' bərn) *adj.* You are **stubborn** when you do not change your mind or give up easily.

earned (ernd') *v.* When you **earned** something, you worked to get it.

successful (sək ses' fəl) *adj.* Someone is **successful** when the person does well.

hobby (hô' bē) *n.* A **hobby** is an activity you like to do in your free time.

tuition (tə wi' shən) *n.* **Tuition** is the money a student pays for classes at a school or college.

Felipe's Photos

READ To Find Out — What does Felipe want to do this summer?

Cast of Characters

FELIPE RIOS, 17

RUDY RIOS, his brother, 13

MR. RIOS, their father

Act I, Scene I

(The living room of the Rios family home.)

MR. RIOS: But I thought we had **agreed**. You will not take that **photography course** this summer.

FELIPE: I just wanted to talk to you one more time, Dad. Summer will be here soon. Please listen to me. I want to take that course at City College.

---

agreed decided the same thing
photography about taking pictures with a camera
course class

MR. RIOS: Felipe! You're so **stubborn**! We've been arguing about this for weeks. Enough!

RUDY: Are you joking? It's been months. Give up, Felipe. I'm tired of hearing about it.

FELIPE: This is not your problem, Rudy. This is between Dad and me.

RUDY: I'm just trying to help. Who would want to go to college in the summer anyway? You're only a junior in high school. My big brother! He doesn't even know what grade he is in!

FELIPE: You are not helping me much, Rudy! Listen, I want to take a photography course. City College will allow a high school student to take the course. I will earn high school **credit**, not college credit.

---

stubborn does not change his ideas
credit proof that he has passed the course

MR. RIOS: You can take a college course, but not in photography. You can take a course that will help you learn about **business**.

RUDY: Why do you want to take this photography course, Felipe? You take millions of photos all the time now. Why do you need to learn how to take more?

FELIPE: Be quiet, Rudy. What do you know? OK, I'll answer you. I want to have a **career** in photography.

MR. RIOS: You **earned** good grades in most of your subjects. You will be able to own a business someday. Take a course in business. Anybody can take a picture! Photography is **hobby**, not a career.

---

business office work
career the main work you plan to do in your life
earned worked to get
hobby an activity people do in their free time

MR. RIOS: I have decided, Felipe. If I am going to pay for your **tuition**, then I make the decision what course you will take.

FELIPE: I have an idea! I can work at Rios **Real Estate**! You have a **successful** business. I'll learn from you how to sell homes to people. I won't have to take a business course.

MR. RIOS: Will you use what I pay you for the photography course?

FELIPE: Yes, I will.

MR. RIOS: Then you will not work at Rios Real Estate. You will not take the photography course either.

(*Mr. Rios's cell phone rings. He answers it.*)

MR. RIOS: I have to go to the office now. Felipe, make your decision tonight. I do not want to talk about this any more.

> **LET'S TALK!** What problem does Felipe have?

---

tuition the money a student must pay for classes at a school or college
real estate a business to help people sell and buy homes
successful has done well

305

READ To Find Out Who helps Felipe?

Act 1, Scene II

(*Rudy and Felipe are in the room they share. Felipe holds photographs he has taken.*)

RUDY: Have you showed Dad your photos?

FELIPE: Sure, but he doesn't really see them.

RUDY: What do you mean?

FELIPE: Well, to him they're **ordinary** photos. For me, they show my **imagination**. They are art.

RUDY: Well, you need to show him your greatest pictures. Show him how you work on our computer to make them look better.

FELIPE: How can I have more time on our computer? You're always playing on-line video games!

RUDY: I'll play at my friend's house for a few days. Brothers have to help each other, right?

ordinary normal; average
imagination creative or original thinking

FELIPE: You sound like you like my photos.

RUDY: I like the photos you took of me on my skateboard. You made me look like I was flying.

FELIPE: Thanks, but that won't help me to **convince** Dad.

RUDY: I already told you. Show him the pictures!

FELIPE: What pictures?

RUDY: I told you, Felipe. You took a million photos. Find great ones that Dad will like. And hurry. He's coming home soon.

FELIPE: It's my turn to make dinner tonight.

RUDY: I'll take your turn this time. Then you can work.

FELIPE: It's a good thing that I'm not very hungry tonight. OK, I'll start working.

---

convince make someone think the way you do

Act 1, Scene III

(*Mr. Rios and Rudy are the kitchen.*)

MR. RIOS: Where is your brother, Rudy?

RUDY: Felipe is in our room. I'm making dinner tonight, Dad.

MR. RIOS: What do you plan to cook, Rudy? Are we having soup from a can and a plate of carrot sticks? That is what Felipe would **serve**.

RUDY: Get ready for the meal of your life, Dad. We will have a mixed green salad with tomatoes and onions. We'll have roasted chicken, beans, and rice. I didn't cook it all, but I know how to serve it. Someday, I want to be a great **chef**.

MR. RIOS: One son wants to be a photographer. The other son wants to be a chef! Where is the son who wants to learn about business?

> **LET'S TALK!** What is Felipe's plan?

---

serve put food on the table
chef someone who cooks in a restaurant

READ
To Find Out

How is Felipe
like his father?

Act 2, Scene I

(*Mr. Rios, Felipe, and Rudy are in the living room.*)

FELIPE: I want you to see the photos as you should see them, Dad.

MR. RIOS: (*Shaking his head*) How did you become so stubborn?

FELIPE: I don't know, Dad. Maybe I'm like you.

MR. RIOS: I've seen some already. Why should I look at them again?

FELIPE: Yes, but you did not see them like this, on the computer.

MR. RIOS: You will never give up, will you?

FELIPE: That's how you taught us to act, Dad.

MR. RIOS: What do you mean, I taught you?

FELIPE: You've always taught us to stand up for what we think is right.

RUDY: Felipe is right, Dad. Do you remember when I didn't make the basketball team last year? You made me practice more, and I made the team this year.

FELIPE: Do you remember when I was having a hard time with math? You sat down and worked with me. Then I passed with a B. You've always showed us how to work for what we want.

MR. RIOS: OK, I think I am beginning to understand. What do you want me to look at, Felipe?

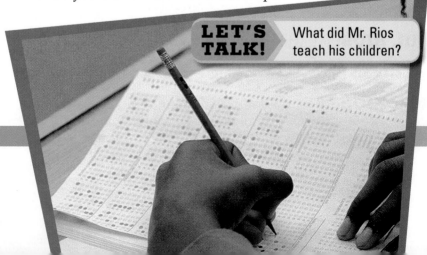

LET'S TALK! What did Mr. Rios teach his children?

READ
To Find Out

What does Felipe find out about his father?

Act 2, Scene II

(Felipe, Rudy, and Mr. Rios are in the boys' room by the computer.)

RUDY: Felipe is just doing what he learned from you, Dad.

MR. RIOS: You mean that you boys have been listening to your father all these years? Felipe, you are doing this because you want to take that photography course this summer, right?

FELIPE: Yes! Didn't you ever fight for a dream?

MR. RIOS: Well, I think it's time to share my little **secret**.

FELIPE: You have a secret?

MR. RIOS: A long time ago, I wanted to be an artist. I thought that I could paint pictures.

RUDY: You mean you wanted to be a real artist like Pablo Picasso?

MR. RIOS: Yes, I wanted to be a real artist.

---

secret something he did not want others to know

311

FELIPE: I never knew that, Dad.

RUDY: What other secrets do you have, Dad?

FELIPE: Rudy, be quiet! What happened, Dad?

MR. RIOS: I had started to work with Aunt Lucy in her real estate business. I had to take many courses, but I had extra time. I began to paint. Then I read about an art fair that the city was planning. I chose my six best **paintings**. Then I paid $25.00 to enter them in the fair. I sold one painting for $180.00! Then I was sure I could be a successful artist.

FELIPE: Wow! You had dreams too!

LET'S TALK! What is Mr. Rios's secret?

---

paintings pictures that an artist makes with paints

READ
To Find Out

What other secret do the kids know?

MR. RIOS: Oh, there's a lot about parents that children don't know. Parents were young once, you know.

RUDY: Did you become a painter?

MR. RIOS: I tried for a while but I didn't sell many paintings. I needed more **training** and education. To tell the truth, I was more successful in business.

FELIPE: That won't happen to me!

MR. RIOS: Are you sure? Felipe, listen to me. I'm just trying to **protect** you. You will be successful in business too.

RUDY: Felipe, I think it's time to show Dad the photos.

---

training classes and practice with a teacher
protect keep something bad from happening

(*Mr. Rios and the boys begin to look at the computer.*)

FELIPE: Here is a photo that I took of some of the buildings in the city.

MR. RIOS: I see the way you show the sunlight shining on those tall buildings. Not bad, Son!

FELIPE: Here is one at the museum. See the statue of the lion?

MR. RIOS: How did you take such a clear photo Felipe? I see so many details.

FELIPE: This one is a close-up. I was at the farmer's market downtown, so I took a photo.

RUDY: The red apples look real! I could take a bite right now.

LET'S TALK! What happens after Mr. Rios tells his secret?

READ To Find Out   Does Felipe convince his dad?

FELIPE: Now, look at these!

MR. RIOS: You took photos of ordinary houses. Those houses look beautiful in your photos.

FELIPE: Dad, I could take pictures of houses that people want to buy. You could use them in your business. I could take pictures of any house for you.

MR. RIOS: You're right, Felipe. These are good photos. I would be happy to use these in my business. Maybe you can help me.

FELIPE: Dad, when you wanted to be an artist, you wanted to have more training. I do too. I want to take the photography course at City College this summer! Will you let me now?

MR. RIOS: I know how hard it is to paint a good picture. It's hard to take good photos like these. Felipe, you convinced me. You should take that photography course.

FELIPE: Thanks, Dad! City College, get ready! The great Felipe Rios is coming!

RUDY: Dad, I have a question.

MR. RIOS: What is it, son?

RUDY: Do you think you'll let me go to cooking school someday?

MR. RIOS: First, you'll have to find a way to convince me.

RUDY: That will be easy! Dad, I was the one who told Felipe how to convince you!

(FELIPE takes his camera and starts to take a picture of RUDY and MR. RIOS.)

What Do You Think? What dreams do you have? How can you help people understand your dreams? Use the sentence frames below. Talk about your ideas with a partner.

Some dreams that I have are ___.
I can help people understand my dreams by ___.

WORKING FOR THE WORLD

Talk About It!

What does being a leader mean to you?

READ • Kofi Annan

Reading Skill **Distinguish Fact and Opinion**

A fact is information that you can prove. An opinion is what someone thinks or feels. Opinions cannot be proven. When you distinguish fact and opinion, you decide which statements are facts and which are opinions. As you read, ask yourself:

❯ Can I find this information in a reference source?

❯ Does this sound like someone's own thoughts or feelings?

You will be able to decide what to believe in a text when you can tell facts from opinions.

As you read, complete the graphic organizer in the *Expressions Practice Book.*

Statement	Fact or Opinion?	Why?

Vocabulary for Kofi Annan

Read the words and definitions below.

attended (ə tend′ əd) *v.* If you went to an event, you **attended** it.

award (ə word′) *n.* An **award** is a prize you get when you win or reach a goal.

career (kə rir′) *n.* A **career** is work for pay in a certain area, such as business, medicine, or sports.
Cognate (Spanish) **carrera**

international (in tər nash′ nəl) *adj.* When something is **international**, it is about two or more countries.
Cognate (Spanish) **internacional**

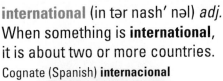

judges (jə′ jəz) *n.* In some contests, **judges** decide who a winner is.
Cognate (Spanish) **jueces**

peaceful (pēs′ fəl) *adj.* Something that is calm and quiet is **peaceful**.
Cognate (Spanish) **pacífico(a)**

cooperation (kō ä′ pə rā′ shən) *n.* **Cooperation** is the act or process of working together.
Cognate (Spanish) **cooperación**

solve (sälv′) *v.* When you **solve** something, you find the answer.
Cognate (Spanish) **resolver**

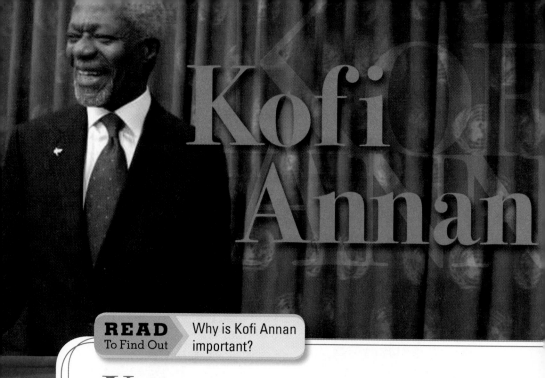

Kofi Annan

READ
To Find Out

Why is Kofi Annan important?

Kofi Annan was the seventh Secretary General of the United Nations. The United Nations (U.N.) is a group of nations, or countries, that work together to **solve** world problems. Kofi Annan was the leader of this **international** group for nine years.

EDUCATION

Kofi Annan was born April 8, 1938, in Kumasi, Ghana. His education began in Ghana, where he **attended** the University of Science and Technology. Then he went to the United States, where he attended Macalester College in St. Paul, Minnesota. He also studied in Geneva, Switzerland. Over the years, Kofi Annan became friends with people from many countries.

---

solve fix; find the answer
international many countries
attended went to

KOFI ANNAN AT THE UNITED NATIONS

In 1962 Kofi Annan began his **career** at the United Nations in Geneva, Switzerland. By this time, Kofi Annan spoke English, French, and many African languages. He had lived in many countries. He had many skills that could help the U.N. reach its goals.

In 1997 Kofi Annan was chosen to lead the U.N. as Secretary General. For the next nine years, he worked hard to make the world a better place.

THE UNITED NATIONS

The United Nations works around the world to
- keep peace inside and between nations.
- help nations work together.
- end poverty.
- build respect for human rights.

LET'S TALK! What does the United Nations do?

career work in a certain area

321

READ
To Find Out

How did Kofi Annan help the countries of Nigeria and East Timor?

SECRETARY GENERAL HELPS NATIONS

Kofi Annan helped many countries around the world. In 1998, Nigeria had a change of government. As Secretary General, Kofi Annan helped the country form a new government in a **peaceful** way.

The next year, Kofi Annan helped a small island near Australia called East Timor. East Timor was trying to become free and **independent** from Indonesia. Kofi Annan worked with East Timor to solve their problems.

In 2000, Kofi Annan stated what he believed were the highest goals of the U.N.— "To work for **equality**. To help end **poverty**. To help end **violence**."

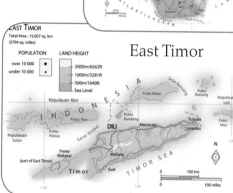

Nigeria

East Timor

peaceful calm; friendly
independent not controlled or ruled by others
equality fair treatment and choices for all people
poverty having too little money to live well
violence harm to people

Kofi Annan Wins the Nobel Peace Prize

Kofi Annan continued to work for peace around the world. In 2001, he won the Nobel Peace Prize. This **award** is given to people who work hard for world peace.

The Nobel Peace prize **judges** said that the United Nations leads the way for peace and **cooperation** in the world. They explained that Kofi Annan helped make the U.N. a better group. Richard Holbrooke, who worked for the United States at the U.N., said Kofi Annan is "the best secretary general in the history of the U.N."

LET'S TALK! Why did Kofi Annan receive the Nobel Peace Prize?

award prize; medal
judges people who choose a winner
cooperation working together

READ To Find Out What did Kofi Annan do after he left the United Nations?

At the United Nations, Annan worked to stop violence in Libya, Nigeria, and other nations around the world.

Kofi Annan worked to help businesses care for the environment.

HIS WORK CONTINUES

Today, Kofi Annan continues his work for world peace. In 2007, he became the leader of **Alliance** for a Green **Revolution** in Africa (AGRA), an organization that helps African farmers.

alliance people or groups working for a shared goal
revolution total change in way of doing something

KOFI ANNAN'S LIFE AND WORK

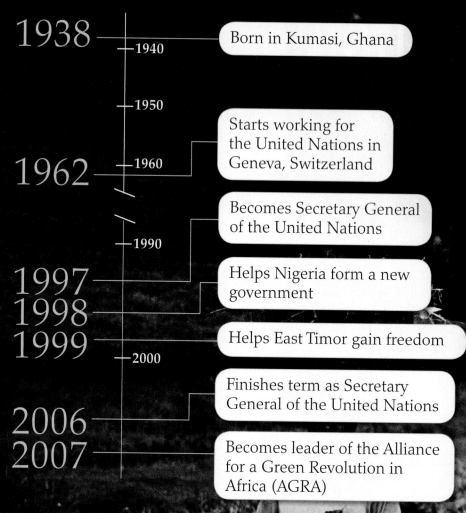

1938 — Born in Kumasi, Ghana

1940

1950

1962 — 1960 — Starts working for the United Nations in Geneva, Switzerland

Becomes Secretary General of the United Nations

1990

1997 — Helps Nigeria form a new government

1998

1999 — Helps East Timor gain freedom

2000

Finishes term as Secretary General of the United Nations

2006

2007 — Becomes leader of the Alliance for a Green Revolution in Africa (AGRA)

What Do You Think? What made Kofi Annan a good leader for the United Nations? With a partner, talk about the qualities a good leader must have. Then write your answers in a web like the one below.

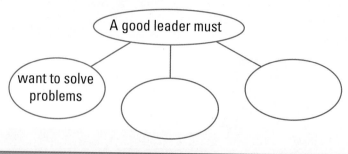

A good leader must

want to solve problems

Don't Give Up

Talk About It!

When do you use your
hands to say things?

READ
- The Debate in
  Sign Language

Literary Element Style

Style is the way an author tells a story.
Sometimes authors use long sentences.
Sometimes their stories have short sentences.
Words are part of style too. Some authors
use many descriptive words. Other authors
use a lot of dialogue. As you read, ask
yourself

> ❯ how long or short are the sentences?
> ❯ what kinds of words does the author use?
> ❯ what descriptions does the author include?
> ❯ does the author include dialogue?

Practice Read the text below. Then choose the phrase that best describes the style of the author's writing.

> Cold, wet, gray fog covered the path. The trees were no more than tall, dark shadows on either side. I looked into the darkness ahead. The lights of my house shone like bright, tiny stars.

1. full of detail   3. full of emotion

2. full of opinion   4. full of dialogue

As you read, complete the graphic organizer in the *Expressions Practice Book*.

The Debate In Sign Language	
	Example From Text
Tone	
Sentence Length	
Descriptive Language	
Figurative Language	

Vocabulary for The Debate in Sign Language

Read the words and definitions below.

astonishing (ə stä′ ni shing) *adj.* Something that is hard to believe and surprises you is **astonishing**.

castle (ka′ səl) *n.* A **castle** is a large stone building where a king and queen live.
Cognate (Spanish) **castillo**

debate (di bāt′) *n.* A **debate** is a talk in which people have two opposite ideas or opinions.
Cognate (Spanish) **debate**

fist (fist′) *n.* When you close your hand tightly together, you make a **fist**.

platform (plat′ form) *n.* A **platform** is a raised area that a person stands on.
Cognate (Spanish) **plataforma**

scattered (ska′ tərd) *v.* Things that are thrown in all different directions are **scattered**.

shrugged (shrəgd′) *v.* You **shrugged** when you raised your shoulders to show you are not sure about something.

surrounded (sə′ raund əd) *v.* Something that is closed in on all sides is **surrounded**.

The Debate in Sign Language

READ To Find Out — Do the Jews get to stay in the land?

by Syd Lieberman

Once there was an evil king who decided he wanted to throw the Jews out of his land. And the way he would do it was this: He would have a **debate** with one of them—in sign language.

He said to the Jewish community, "I will give you three signs. If someone can read my three signs and answer me correctly, all of you can stay here for the rest of your days. But if not, all of your people will have to go."

Well, the Jewish community was **up in arms**. No one knew what to do. There were **arguments** and discussions but no **volunteers**. After all, who could debate a king, let alone debate a king in sign language?

---

debate a talk in which people have opposite ideas
up in arms very upset
arguments talks in which people tell their ideas and sometimes disagree with each other
volunteers people who agree to do something

So, finally, after days of arguments going up and back, Yankel, a little chicken man, said, "Look, if no one will do it, I'll do it." And so the Jews agreed. Off went Yankel to the debate.

A huge **platform** had been set up in the center of town. Everybody **surrounded** it. The king stood on one side, little Yankel on the other. The king said, "Okay, I will give you three signs. If you get them all correct, you can stay with your people in this land. If you don't, all of you will have to leave.

"Here is the first sign."

The king threw an arm in the air and stretched out the fingers of his hand. Yankel looked at the king and put a **fist** in front of his face.

The king said, "Correct. I'm amazed. Here is the second sign."

---

platform high place for a speaker to stand on
surrounded closed in on all sides
fist hand held with fingers curled tight in a ball

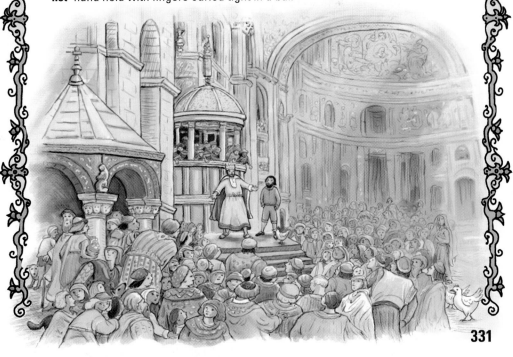

He threw his arm toward Yankel with two fingers straight out, and Yankel put one finger up in front of his nose.

The king said, "Correct again. If you get the third sign right, you and all of your people will be able to **remain**."

And he reached into the folds of his robe and pulled out a piece of cheese. Yankel looked at the king, **shrugged**, and pulled out an egg from his **pouch**.

The king gasped. "Correct again. The Jews can stay!"

LET'S TALK! The king made three signs. What do his signs mean?

remain stay
shrugged raised and lowered shoulders quickly
pouch bag

That night in the **castle** the whole court gathered around the king and asked, "What was the debate about?"

The king replied, "It was **astonishing** that the Jews had a little chicken man who could read my signs. I put out my hand with my fingers spread to show him that the Jews were **scattered** all over the world. But he put up a fist to show me that they were one in the hand of God."

"Then I held up two fingers to show him that there were two kings, one in heaven and one on the earth. But he held up one finger to show me there was only one king in heaven."

"So I brought out a piece of cheese to show the chicken man that the Jewish religion had grown old and moldy, but he brought out an egg to show me that it was fresh and whole."

"It was amazing."

---

castle large, stone home of a king and queen
astonishing hard to believe
scattered tossed or thrown in many different directions

333

Meanwhile, at Yankel's, everybody crowded into the chicken store and asked, "What was the debate about?"

Yankel replied, "I don't know! It wasn't much of a debate. I mean, the king reached out to grab me so I put up a fist to show him I'd punch him if he touched me. Then the king held up two fingers to poke out my eyes, so I held up one to block him. I guess he knew I was going to stand up to him, so he brought out his lunch and I brought out mine!"

What Do You Think? You tell the next part of the story. Someone tells the king Yankel did not really understand the signs. What will the king do? Talk with a partner. Use the sentence frames below.

The king felt _____.

He told Yankel _____.

Now Yankel has to _____.

To Bring Light and Warmth

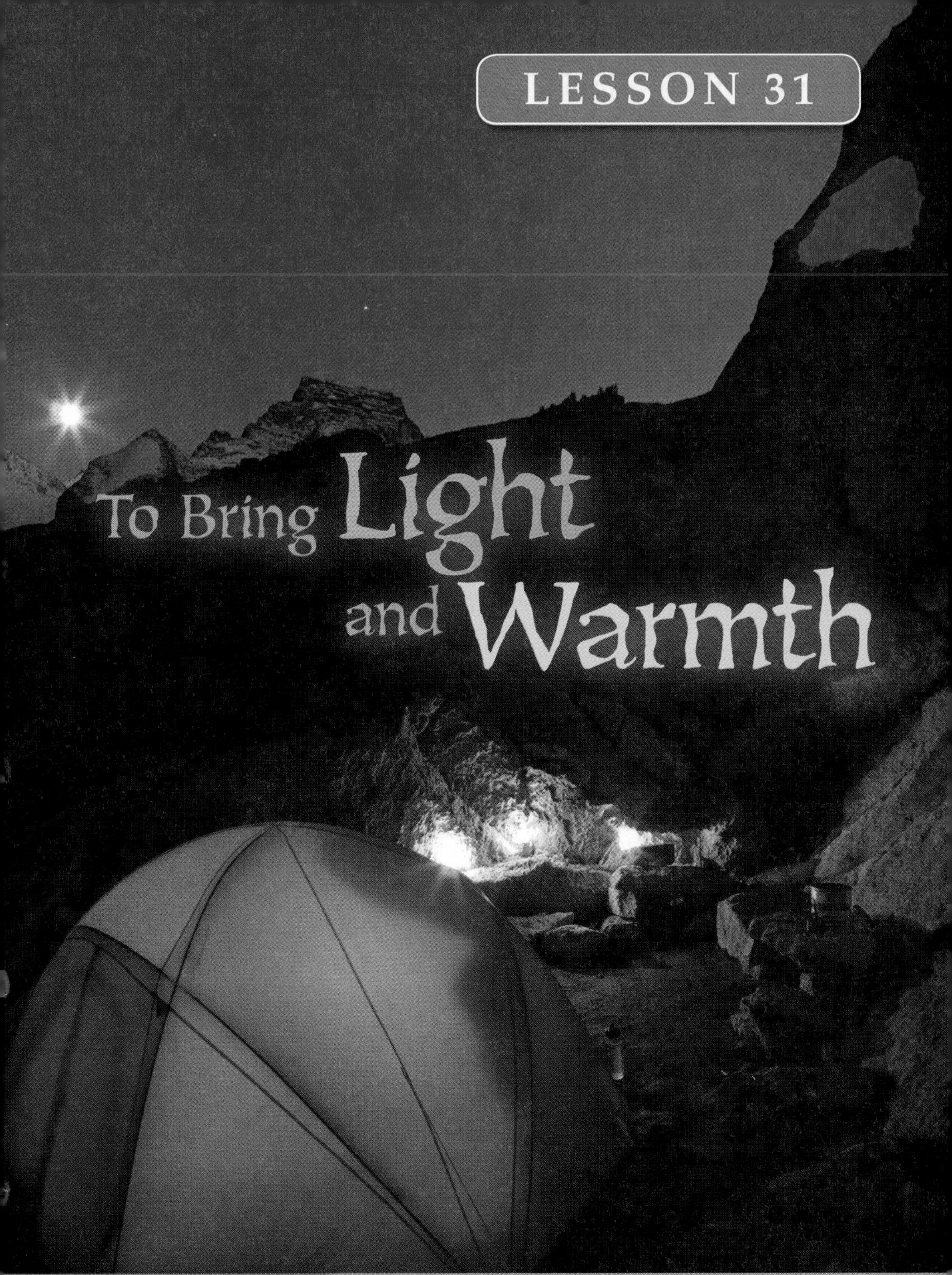

Talk About It!

What would life be like without fire?

READ
- Loo-Wit: The Fire Keeper
- Prometheus and the Fire

Reading Skill **Compare and Contrast Style**

Style is an author's way of writing. Some authors may use detailed descriptions. Others might use simple sentences.

You can **compare and contrast styles** of texts. When you compare styles, you look for ways the styles are alike. When you contrast styles, you find how the styles are different.

Practice Read both paragraphs below. Then talk about the differences with a partner. Make a list of what you find.

Jamal

The pool was empty. Jamal wondered if he could swim across it. He climbed into the pool. He took a deep breath. Then he swam to the other side.

Thanh

Thanh swam like a shiny pink fish in the ocean. She would dive under the water, quickly kick her legs, and splash her arms in the waves. Thanh loved to swim more than anything in the world!

As you read, complete the graphic organizer in the *Expressions Practice Book*.

	Loo-Wit: The Fire Keeper	Prometheus and the Fire
Tone		
Sentence Length		
Descriptive Language		
Figurative Language		

Read the words and definitions below.

argued (är′ gyūd) *v.* When two people have **argued**, they have discussed a strong disagreement.
Cognate (Spanish) **argumentar**

peace (pēs′) *n.* **Peace** is when people live in a friendly way and do not fight.
Cognate (Spanish) **paz**

arrow (er′ ō) *n.* An **arrow** is a sharp pointed stick that someone shoots from a bow.

river (ri′ vər) *n.* A **river** is a large body of moving water.
Cognate (Spanish) **río**

bridge (brij′) *n.* Someone builds a **bridge** so that people cross over the water or land below.

split (split′) *v.* When you break something in two, you **split** it.

crops (kräps′) *n.* **Crops** are fruits, vegetables, or grains that a farmer grows.

storm (storm′) *n.* A **storm** is bad weather, often with strong wind, and rain, snow, or lightning.

LOO-WIT The Fire Keeper

Based on a story by Joseph Bruchac

READ To Find Out
How did Earth used to be?

Long ago, the Creator gave people everything they needed to be happy. The weather was always nice. **Crops** grew tall. There was plenty of food for everyone.

Still, two brothers **argued** over land. Each wanted to rule, to be in charge of the people. The people **split** into two groups. It looked as though there would be war between the groups.

This made the Creator unhappy. One night, when the brothers were asleep, he carried them to a new country. The land was beautiful. A flowing **river** divided the land and mountains rose into the clouds.

The brothers woke as the sun came up. They saw what a good place it was and they were glad. The Creator said, "This will be your land."

---

crops fruits, grains, and vegetables that grow on a farm
argued did not agree with each other
split broke in half; separated
river large body of moving water

338

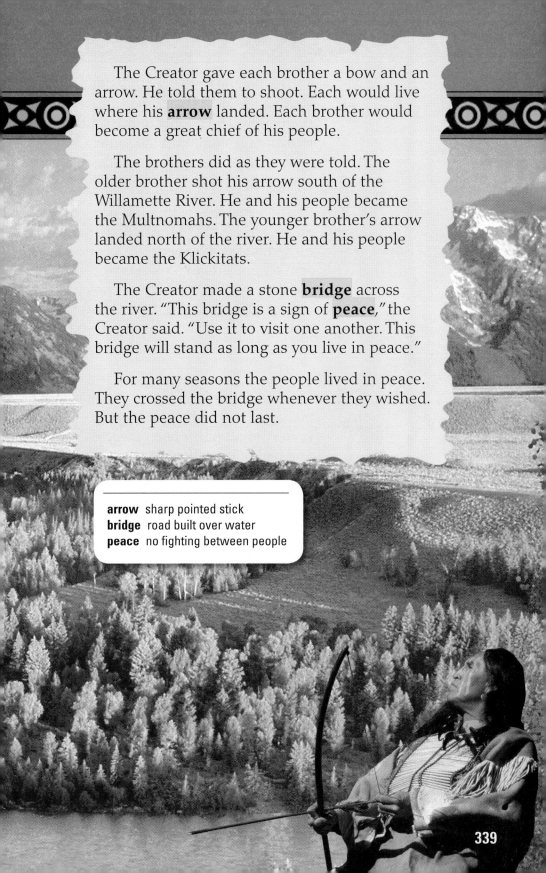

The Creator gave each brother a bow and an arrow. He told them to shoot. Each would live where his **arrow** landed. Each brother would become a great chief of his people.

The brothers did as they were told. The older brother shot his arrow south of the Willamette River. He and his people became the Multnomahs. The younger brother's arrow landed north of the river. He and his people became the Klickitats.

The Creator made a stone **bridge** across the river. "This bridge is a sign of **peace**," the Creator said. "Use it to visit one another. This bridge will stand as long as you live in peace."

For many seasons the people lived in peace. They crossed the bridge whenever they wished. But the peace did not last.

arrow sharp pointed stick
bridge road built over water
peace no fighting between people

The people to the north looked south and said, "Their lands are better than ours." The people to the south looked north and said the same. Once again, the two groups of people began to argue.

The Creator saw this and was angry. The hearts of the people had turned bad with **greed**. The Creator sent a huge **storm** to darken the sky. He took away fire, and the people were cold. They begged the Creator to give them fire again. They promised to live in peace.

At last, the Creator's heart was touched. Fire **remained** in just one place on Earth. An old woman named Loo-Wit had never been greedy. She had never taken sides in the arguments. The Creator offered her whatever she wanted in return for sharing her fire with the people.

LET'S TALK! Why do the Multnomahs and Klickitats argue?

---

greed wanting more than is fair
storm very bad weather
remained stayed

READ To Find Out   What did Loo-Wit want?

Loo-Wit told the Creator that she wanted to be young and beautiful. The Creator agreed. "Take your fire to the bridge," he said. "Let the people get fire from you. The fire must burn always. It will remind the people not to fight."

The next morning, the people woke up to a warm, bright day. They saw a beautiful young woman on the bridge. Loo-Wit gave fire to the people, and they promised to live in peace.

Then the chiefs came to Loo-Wit's fire. When they saw her beauty, both wanted to marry her. They began to fight. Their people joined the battle, and a war began.

The Creator saw this and was furious. He showed his **might**. He broke the stone bridge. He turned each chief into a mountain.

---

might how strong he was

341

The chief of the Klickitats became Mount Adams. The chief of the Multnomahs became Mount Hood. But even as mountains, the chiefs fought. They threw flames and stones at one another. The stones almost blocked the beautiful river.

Loo-Wit's heart fell over the pain her beauty had caused. She no longer wanted to live as a beautiful young woman or even as a human being.

The Creator **pitied** her. He made her into the most beautiful of all mountains. She stood between Mount Adams and Mount Hood. The Creator allowed her to hold the fire from the bridge inside herself to keep peace between the **warring** chiefs. She still holds the fire, and she still tries to keep peace between the people.

---

pitied felt sorry for
warring fighting

What Do You Think? Do you think any people today act like the brothers in this story? Talk with a partner. Use the sentence frame below.

I think that the brothers in this story are like ___ because ___ .

Vocabulary for **Prometheus and the Fire**

Read the words and definitions below.

carefully (ker′ fu lē) *adv.* When you do something **carefully**, you pay attention and do not hurry.

raw (rȯ′) *adj.* Something **raw** is not cooked.

decision (di si′ zhən) *n.* When you make a **decision**, you choose what you will do or not do.

Cognate (Spanish) **decisión**

roasted (rōst′ əd) *v.* When you have **roasted** something, you have cooked it with dry heat.

greedy (grē′ dē) *adj.* When you take more than you need you are **greedy**.

shivering (shi′ və ring) *v.* When you are **shivering**, you are shaking from the cold.

punishment (pə′ nish mənt) *n.* People who commit a crime or do something wrong may have a **punishment**.

worship (wor′ shəp) *v.* When people **worship** something, they honor and obey it as their god.

PROMETHEUS AND THE FIRE

Can you imagine a world without fire? The room you are in might be as cold and dark as a cave. You would have to eat all of your food **raw**. Life would be harder.

Long ago, Prometheus noticed humans didn't have fire. Prometheus was a god on **Mount Olympus** in Greece. He went to complain to Zeus, king of the gods.

"I don't understand your plan," Prometheus said to Zeus. "Look at the humans below the mountain. They are **shivering** in the cold and they can't even see each other at night! Why won't you give fire to the humans?"

Zeus had reasons. "Every gift has a cost. A fire that heats a home can also destroy a home. Besides, humans are happy without fire," he replied.

---

raw not cooked
Mount Olympus tall mountain in Greece
shivering shaking from the cold

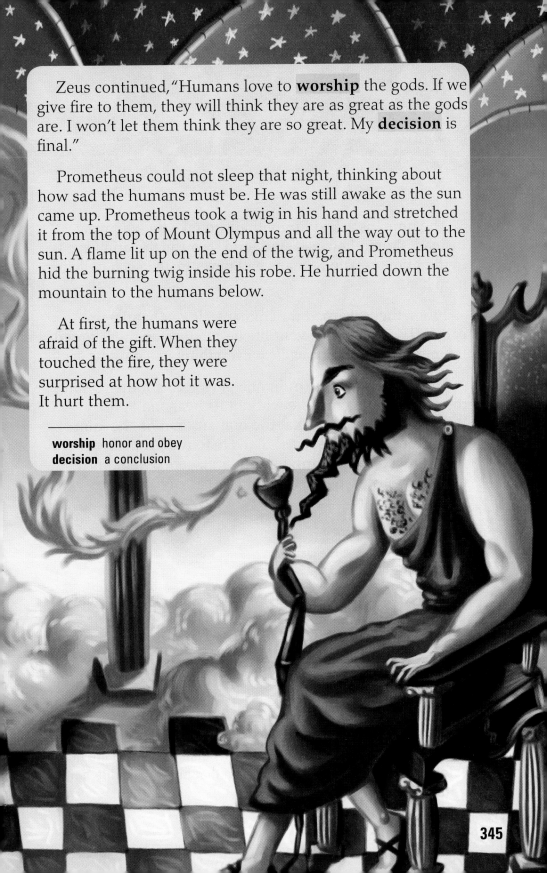

Zeus continued, "Humans love to **worship** the gods. If we give fire to them, they will think they are as great as the gods are. I won't let them think they are so great. My **decision** is final."

Prometheus could not sleep that night, thinking about how sad the humans must be. He was still awake as the sun came up. Prometheus took a twig in his hand and stretched it from the top of Mount Olympus and all the way out to the sun. A flame lit up on the end of the twig, and Prometheus hid the burning twig inside his robe. He hurried down the mountain to the humans below.

At first, the humans were afraid of the gift. When they touched the fire, they were surprised at how hot it was. It hurt them.

worship honor and obey
decision a conclusion

The humans asked Prometheus to take the gift away. Instead, Prometheus **roasted** food over the fire and gave it to the humans. The humans had never tasted such delicious food before.

Prometheus warned the humans. "If you handle fire **carefully**, it can make your life better. But the fire is **greedy**. If fire grows too big, it will eat everything in sight," he said.

Humans passed fire from one person to another. Soon, they couldn't imagine life without its heat and light. When Zeus found out that the humans had fire he knew Prometheus had disobeyed him. He found Prometheus and gave him a terrible **punishment**. Still, people tell this myth to remember Prometheus and his great gift of fire.

---

roasted cooked
carefully slowly and with attention
greedy taking more than needed
punishment a hard thing to do

What Do You Think? In this story, humans did not want fire at first. But then they saw how it could help make life better. Talk with a partner about something that helps make life better. How does it help?

At first ____ did not want to ____. Later, ____.

▲ Writing Workshop

Writing That Explains
What are your lifetime goals? Think about something worthwhile that you would like to do in your life. Can you do it now? If not, what do you have to do to achieve your goal?

Writing Assignment
For this Writing Workshop, you will write an **expository essay** about one of your goals. You will explain why the goal is important and how you plan to accomplish it. Write your essay for your classmates and your teacher. They will be your audience.

WRITING PLAN

> Present the **thesis**, or main idea, in the introduction.

> Organize the essay around three or four supporting ideas that are well thought out.

> Use interesting language to keep the reader's interest.

> End the essay by restating the thesis from the first paragraph.

Writing Model
Read the student model below.

My life's goal is to become a doctor. When I was seven years old, I broke my arm. The doctors thought that I might not be able to bend my arm again. Dr. Steven Moore operated on my arm. Today, I can play baseball and lift and carry things. I know now that I want to become a doctor. I want to help others like Dr. Moore helped me.

Prewrite

1. **Gather Ideas**

   To get started on your expository essay, think about how people you know have achieved their goals. Read through any journals or diaries. Think about people you admire. Then spend some time thinking about your own future. Make a list of goals that you would like to achieve.

2. **Choose a Goal**

   Review your list. Choose a goal that you think is important. Think of the ways you can reach your goal yourself. Also think of the people who can help you reach your goal. Then write a thesis statement explaining why you chose the goal you did. Use the sentence frame below.

   I have a goal of ___ because ___.

3. **Get Organized**

   Use your notes to create a **flowchart** showing the steps you will take to reach your goal. List reasons for each step and anyone who might help you.

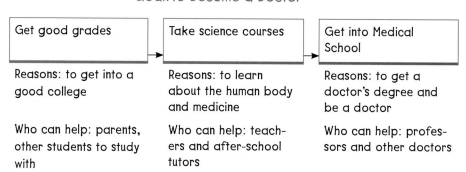

Goal: To Become a Doctor

Get good grades	Take science courses	Get into Medical School

Reasons: to get into a good college

Who can help: parents, other students to study with

Reasons: to learn about the human body and medicine

Who can help: teachers and after-school tutors

Reasons: to get a doctor's degree and be a doctor

Who can help: professors and other doctors

Draft

1. **Start Writing**
   Review your thesis statement and your flowchart. Your flowchart is your guide. Use it to help you decide what to write.

2. **Add to Your Draft**
   Think of the essay as a **step-by-step** guide to reach your goal. Start by writing a thesis statement that tells what your goal is. Include it in the first paragraph.

   > I know now that I want to become a doctor. I want to help others like Dr. Moore helped me.

   Order your essay into the steps you will take to reach your goal. Include your reasons for following each step.

   > I'm already taking the first step. I study hard in school so that I can go to a good college.

   Restate your thesis in your last paragraph.

   > Being a doctor is my dream. I am taking steps right now to make my dream come true.

USE GOOD WRITING TRAITS: IDEAS

The main idea of your essay is what the essay is mainly about. As you draft your essay, make sure you present a clear main idea and supporting details that make sense.

Read the following example. Identify the important details that will help readers remember the main idea.

> To be a doctor, I have to go to medical school. There, I will take science courses because they will help me understand the human body.

Read your essay aloud. Ask yourself: Will my readers remember my goal? Have I included important details?

Revise

Now it's time to revise your draft. This step helps you make your writing better so that others will want to read it.

1. **Read Your Expository Essay** Ask yourself these questions:
   - Does the introductory paragraph include a thesis statement?
   - Does the essay have details and examples supporting the main idea?
   - Are any steps toward the goal missing?

2. **Show Your Expository Essay** Trade drafts with a partner. Answer these questions as you read your partner's essay.
   - Can you tell what the goal of the writer is?
   - Is the main idea supported by details and examples?
   - Do the steps toward the goal make sense?
   - Does the conclusion restate the thesis and make a good ending?

3. **Make Your Changes** Talk with your partner to help you decide what changes you need to make. Then revise your draft.

> **Technology** Use the design features of your word processing software to add or create graphics that can show the steps you follow in a process. Use letters, numbers, or even colors to separate the steps. You can also include pictures and photos that show why your goal is important.

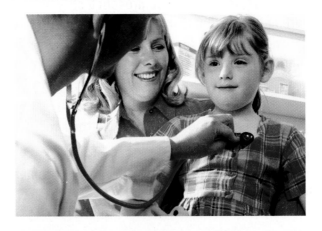

Edit and Proofread

1. **Proofread Your Essay** Reread your expository essay. Look for mistakes in capitalization, punctuation, or spelling. Use the proofreading symbols chart on page 353 to mark changes.

2. **Check Your Sentences** Did you use complete sentences? Do subjects and verbs agree? Make changes if you need to.

Grammar Focus: Appositives

An **appositive** is a word or phrase that follows a noun or pronoun and renames it. An appositive adds new information.

Problem: It is not clear which words rename the noun.

> Dr. Steven Moore a talented surgeon operated on my arm.

Solution: Place commas around the appositive. You can remove an appositive without changing the meaning of the sentence.

> Dr. Steven Moore, a talented surgeon, operated on my arm.

Problem: The sentences are choppy and do not flow well.

> Josie's sister can tell me about good medical schools. Josie's sister is studying to be a doctor in college.

Solution: Notice that each sentence adds new information about Josie's sister. Combine the sentences using an appositive.

> Josie's sister, a pre-med major in college, knows about medical schools and can tell me about good ones.

3. **Make a Final Copy** Make the corrections that you marked. If you are working on the computer, print out the corrected work. If not, rewrite it.

Present

Here are some ways to share your writing.

- Give your essay to your friends to read and ask them for their comments.
- Have a friend read your essay and tell you how he or she would try to reach the goal you wrote about in your essay.

🔊 Speaking, Listening, and Viewing Workshop

Active Listening and Note-Taking

Activity

1. **What is Active Listening?**
   In a **group discussion**, you should listen carefully to what other people are saying. Then you should think about what you heard before speaking. This process is called **active listening**.

2. **Why is Active Listening Important?**
   Active listening is important because listening to others helps you learn. You might find out something you didn't know about. Or it might help you understand a confusing idea.

3. **How Do I Do It?**
   To actively listen, start by focusing on the speaker's words. What words did the speaker choose? Do they have special meaning? Take notes on any important or new information. Make an outline from your notes and write down any questions you might have for the speaker. Use the following sentence frames to help you:
   - I'm confused about ___. Will you explain that more clearly?
   - I disagree with ___ because ___. Has your opinion changed?
   - Based on what you've said, ___ must be true. Do you agree?

4. **Active Listening and Note-Taking Checklist**
   - Did you identify the speaker's purpose?
   - Did you understand the speaker's tone and body language?
   - Did you write down the speaker's main points?
   - Did you ask questions to make information clearer?

Listening to Learn
Take notes as you listen. When it is your turn to talk, use your notes and sentence frames to ask the speaker questions.
   - I believe your main point is ___. Is that correct?
   - I disagree with you about ___. What about this position: ___?

PROOFREADING MARKS

Proofreading Checklist

☑ Have I avoided run-on sentences and sentence fragments?

☑ Have I used every word correctly, including frequently confused words and homophones?

☑ Have I formed plural and possessive nouns correctly?

☑ Do verbs agree with their subjects? Are verb tenses correct? Does verb tense shift correctly to show sequence of events?

☑ Do pronouns refer clearly to their antecedents and agree with them in person, number, and gender?

☑ Have adjective and adverb forms been used correctly?

☑ Have I avoided or corrected dangling participles and misplaced modifiers?

☑ Are all words spelled correctly? Has every unfamiliar word been checked in a dictionary?

☑ Are all punctuation marks used correctly?

Proofreading Symbols

⊙	Lieut Brown	Insert a period.
∧	No one came to the party.	Insert a letter or a word.
∧	The bell rang the students left for home.	Insert a semicolon.
≡	I enjoyed paris.	Capitalize a letter.
/	The Class ran a bake sale.	Make a capital letter lowercase.
⌢	The campers are home sick.	Close up a space.
sp	They visited N.Y. sp	Spell out.
∧	Sue please help.	Insert a comma.
∩	He enjoyed feild day.	Transpose the position of letters or words.
#	alltogether	Insert a space.
ℐ	We went to to Boston.	Delete letters or words.
∨ ∨	She asked, Who's coming?	Insert quotation marks.
/ = /	mid January	Insert a hyphen.
¶	"Where?" asked Karl. "Over there," said Ray.	Begin a new paragraph.
∨	She liked Sarah's glasses.	Insert an apostrophe.

This glossary lists the vocabulary words found in the selections in this book. The definition given is for the word as it is used in the selection; you may wish to consult a dictionary for other meanings of these words. The key below is a guide to the pronunciation symbols used in each entry.

Pronunciation Key

a	**a**t	ō	h**o**pe	ng	si**ng**		
ā	**a**pe	ô	f**o**rk, **a**ll	th	**th**in		
ä	f**a**ther	oo	w**oo**d, p**u**t	<u>th</u>	**th**is		
e	**e**nd	ōō	f**oo**l	zh	trea**s**ure		
ē	m**e**	oi	**oi**l	ə	**a**go, tak**e**n, penc**i**l,		
i	**i**t	ou	**ou**t		lem**o**n, circ**u**s		
ī	**i**ce	u	**u**p	′	indicates primary stress		
o	h**o**t	ū	**u**se	′	indicates secondary stress		

English

Espanõl

A

A

accent (′ak sent) *n.* a way of speaking

accent/acento *s.* una manera de hablar

active (′ak tiv) *adj.* busy working and doing many things

active/activo *adj.* ocupado trabajando y haciendo otras cosas

admired (əd mīrd′) *v.* wanted to be like

admired/admiraba *v.* quería ser igual

adult (ə ′dəlt) *n.* full grown person or animal

adult/adulto *s.* persona o animal que ha crecido por completo

age (′āj) *n.* number of years since birth

age/edad *s.* número de años desde el nacimiento

amazed (ə′ māzd) *v.* surprised

amazed/asombró *v.* sorprendió

amphitheatres (ˈam pə thē ə tərs) *n.* outdoor theaters

ancient (ānˈ shənt) *adj.* very old

archeologists (är kē äˈlə jists) *n.* people who study fossils

argued (ˈär gyüd) *v.* did not agree with each other

arrested (ə resˈ təd) *v.* took people to jail

arrow (ˈar ō) *n.* sharp pointed stick

astonishing (ə stäˈ ni shing) *adj.* surprising, impressing

attack (ə takˈ) *v.* using force to hurt someone or something

attended (ə tendˈ əd) *v.* went to

autumn (oˈ təm) *n.* the season between summer and winter

award (ə wordˈ) *n.* prize; medal

awareness (ə werˈnəs) *n.* information

B

bakes (bāksˈ) *v.* makes it very hot

ballot (baˈlət) *n.* where you mark your choice when you vote

bank (baŋkˈ) *n.* strip of land by a river

bill (bilˈ) *v.* send a letter to ask for money

bleed (blēd) *v.* to lose or leak blood

boil (boi əlˈ) *v.* cook in very hot water

---

amphitheatres/anfiteatros *s.* teatros al aire libre

ancient/antiguo *adj.* muy viejo

archeologists/arqueólogos *s.* personas que estudian fósiles

argued/discutieron *v.* no se pusieron de acuerdo

arrested/arrestó *v.* llevó a alguien a la cárcel

arrow/flecha *s.* palo puntiagudo

astonishing/asombroso *adj.* sorprendente, impresionante

attack/atacar *v.* usar la fuerza para lastimar a alguien o algo

attended/asistió *v.* fue

autumn/otoño *s.* la estación entre el verano y el invierno

award/premio *s.* galardón; medalla

awareness/conciencia *s.* información

B

bakes/cocer *v.* hacer muy caliente

ballot/papeleta *s.* papel donde uno marca su elección al votar

bank/ribera *s.* franja de tierra que está cerca de un río

bill/facturar *v.* enviar una carta para pedir dinero

bleed/sangrar *v.* perder o brotar sangre

boil/hervir *v.* cocer en agua muy caliente

bridge ('brij) *n.* road built over water

bridge/puente *s.* camino construido sobre el agua

C

C

career (kə rir') *n.* work in a certain area

career/carrera *s.* trabajo en determinada área

career (kə rir) *n.* the main work you plan to do in your life

career/carrera *s.* el principal trabajo que uno planea realizar en la vida

castle (ka' səl) *n.* large, stone home of a king and queen

castle/castillo *s.* casa grande de piedra de un rey y una reina

catch (kach') *v.* capture

catch/apresar *v.* capturar

cattle (ka' təl) *n.* cows and bulls

cattle/ganado *s.* vacas y toros

celebrate (se' lə brāt) *v.* have a party and give thanks

celebrate/festejar *v.* tener una fiesta y dar gracias

celebration (se' lə brā shən) *n.* a party to give thanks

celebration/celebración *s.* una fiesta para dar gracias

challenge (cha' lənj) *n.* offer of a contest

challenge/desafío *s.* propuesta de una prueba

cleverness ('kle vər nəs) *n.* tricks for solving problems

cleverness/astucia *s.* trucos para resolver problemas

climate (klī'mət) *n.* average weather

climate/clima *s.* condiciones regulares del tiempo

coasts (kōsts') *n.* lands at the edge of oceans

coasts/costas *s.* tierras que están en la orilla de los océanos

confident (kän' fə dent) *adj.* sure

confident/confiado *adj.* seguro

conflict (kän' flikt) *n.* strong disagreement

conflict/conflicto *s.* fuerte desacuerdo

connects (kə nekts') *v.* becomes joined together

connects/conecta *v.* une, junta

conquered (käə'kərd) *v.* won a war against

conquered/conquistó *v.* ganó una guerra

contest (kən'test) *n.* a game or a race to see who can win

contest/prueba *s.* un juego o una carrera para ver quién puede ganar

convince (kən 'vin(t) s) *v.* make someone believe

convince/convencer *v.* hacer creer a alguien

convinced (kən vinsd") v. made someone believe something

cooperation (kō ä pə rā' shən) n. working together

costumes (käs¦tümz) n. masks and clothing that actors wear on a stage

countryside (kən-trē-¦sīd ') n. open land for farms and animals

courage (kur' ij) adj. not having fear when there is danger

crate (krāt') n. box for carrying objects

crime (krīm') n. an action that breaks the law

crops ('kräps) n. fruits, grains, and vegetables that grow on a farm

crops ('kräps) n. plants that people grow for food

crowd (kraud') n. group

crowded (kraud' əd) adj. having too many people

crushed ('krəshd') v. pushed down and hurt

custom (kəs' təm) n. a tradition

cyclone (sī' klōn) n. a tornado, spinning winds that form a funnel

D

dangerous (dān'jə rəs) adj. something that hurts people or things

debate (di bāt') n. a talk in which people have opposing ideas

convinced/convenció v. hizo que alguien creyera algo

cooperation/cooperación s. trabajar juntos

costumes/disfraces s. máscaras y ropa que los actores se ponen en el escenario

countryside/campo s. amplio terreno que se usa para labrar o criar animales

courage/valiente adj. que no tiene miedo en caso de peligro

crate/cajón s. caja grande para llevar cosas

crime/crimen s. una acción que viola la ley

crops/cosechas s. frutas, granos y verduras que se cultivan en una granja

crops/cultivos s. plantas que la gente siembra para comer

crowd/muchedumbre s. grupo

crowded/atestado adj. tener demasiada gente

crushed/aplastó v. empujó y lastimó

custom/costumbre s. tradición

cyclone/ciclón s. un tornado, vientos que dan vueltas y forman un embudo

D

dangerous/peligroso adj. algo que lastima a la gente o las cosas

debate/debate s. conversación en la que las personas tienen ideas opuestas

debating (di bāt'iŋ) *v.* discussing facts and opinions with others

decorate (de'kə ˌrāt) *v.* to make pretty

desires (di-'zīrz) *n.* strong wishes for things

disagree (ˌdis ə grē') *v.* have different opinions about

disclose (dis klōz') *v.* let others know

discriminated (dis kri'mə nā təd) *v.* treated unfairly

disease (di zēz') *n.* illness

disease (di-zēz) *n.* sickness

disrespectful (dis ri spekt' fəl) *adj.* rude

dragged (dragd') *v.* pulled

drama (drä' mə) *n.* a play or story that is acted on a stage

dynasty (dī'nə stē) *n.* line of rulers from one family

debating/debatir *v.* discutir hechos y opiniones con los demás

decorate/decorar *v.* hacer bonito

desires/deseos *s.* fuertes ganas de algo

disagree/diferir *v.* tener opiniones diferentes

disclose/revelar *v.* decir a los demás

discriminated/discriminó *v.* trató de manera injusta

disease/padecimiento *s.* enfermedad

disease/enfermedad *s.* dolencia

disrespectful/irrespetuoso *adj.* grosero

dragged/arrastró *v.* tiró de

drama/drama *s.* una obra o historia que se representa en un escenario

dynasty/dinastía *s.* serie de gobernantes que pertenecen a una familia

E

E

earned ('ərnd) *v.* worked to get

earning ('ər niŋ) *v.* being paid

elders (el' dərz) *n.* people who are older than you

elect (i lekt') *v.* to choose a leader

emperor (em'pər ər) *n.* male ruler

enormous (i nor' məs) *adj.* very large

earned/ganó *v.* trabajó para obtener

earning/ganar *v.* recibir un pago

elders/mayores *s.* personas que tienen más edad que tú

elect/elegir *v.* escoger a un líder

emperor/emperador *s.* gobernante masculino

enormous/enorme *adj.* muy grande

equal (ē' kwəl) *adj.* the same

equality (i kwä'lə tē) *n.* the same opportunities for everyone

escape (is kāp') *v.* get away from

example (ig zam'pəl) *n.* a model for what someone else does

excited (ik sī' təd) *v.* looking forward to

excitement (ik sīt' mənt) *n.* happiness

expensive (ik spen' siv) *adj.* something that costs a lot of money

equal/igual *adj.* el mismo

equality/igualdad *s.* las mismas oportunidades para todos

escape/escapar *v.* salir de

example/ejemplo *s.* una muestra de lo que hace otra persona

excited/emocionado *adv.* esperar algo con ansiedad

excitement/emoción *s.* felicidad

expensive/caro *adj.* algo que cuesta mucho dinero

F

F

fame (fām) *n.* being well known by many

famous (fā' məs) *adj.* popular; well-known

famous (fā'məs) *adj.* well-known

fangs (fangz') *n.* sharp teeth

farm (färm') *n.* land for growing plants and keeping animals

feathers (fe' thərz) *n.* what covers a bird's body

ferocious (fə rō' shəs) *adj.* mean

festivals (fes'tə vəl) *v.* celebrations

fields (fēldz') *n.* land used for growing crops

fiercely (firs' lē) *adv.* like a fighter would

fist (fist') *n.* hand held with fingers curled tight in a ball

flames (flāmz') *n.* burning fire

fame/fama *s.* ser bien conocido por mucha gente

famous/famoso *adj.* popular; bien conocido

famous/famoso *adj.* bien conocido

fangs/colmillos *s.* dientes filosos

farm/granja *s.* terreno para cultivar plantas y criar animales

feathers/plumas *s.* lo que cubre el cuerpo de los pájaros

ferocious/feroz *adj.* malo

festivals/festivales *s.* celebraciones

fields/campos *s.* tierra que se usa para sembrar cultivos

fiercely/ferozmente *adv.* como lo haría un luchador

fist/puño *s.* cerrar la mano con los dedos doblados hacia adentro

flames/llamas *s.* fuego, incendio

follow ('fä-lō) *v.* to be guided by something

forest (for' əst) *n.* an area with many trees

funnel (f ə'n əl) *n.* an object that is wide at one end, and narrow at the other

follow/seguir *v.* ser guiado por algo

forest/bosque *s.* un área con muchos árboles

funnel/embudo *s.* un objeto que es ancho de un lado y estrecho del otro

G

gather (ga' thər) *v.* come together

glaciers (glā'shərz) *n.* large sheets of ice

goggles (gä'gəlz) *n.* something to wear over the eyes to protect them

grateful (grāt' fəl) *adj.* thankful for something

guardian (gär' dē ən) *n.* person who is responsible for someone else

G

gather/reunir *v.* juntar

glaciers/glaciares *s.* grandes capas de hielo

goggles/gafas *(protectoras)* *s.* algo que se pone sobre los ojos para protegerlos

grateful/agradecido *adj.* que muestra gratitud por algo

guardian/guardián *s.* persona que es responsable por alguien más

H

harness (här'nəs) *n.* straps to control an animal

healthy (hel' thē) *adj.* not sick

heroes (hir' ōz) *n.* People who do great things

hiss (his') *v.* to make a sound like air coming out of a tire

hobby (hä ' bē) *n.* an activity people do in their free time

honest (ä' nəst) *adj.* people who follow the law

honor (ä'nər) *v.* help others remember someone important or loved

H

harness/arnés *s.* correas para controlar a un animal

healthy/sano *adj.* que no está enfermo

heroes/héroes *s.* personas que hacen cosas extraordinarias

hiss/silbar *v.* producir un sonido como de aire que sale de una rueda

hobby/pasatiempo *s.* la actividad que uno realiza en su tiempo libre

honest/honrado *adj.* persona que obedece la ley

honor/honrar *v.* ayudar a los demás recordar a alguien importante o a un ser querido

household (haủsˈˌhōld) *n.* a group or family living together

humidity (hyü miˈdə tē) *n.* water in the air

hunting (hənˈting) *v.* looking for

household/hogar *s.* un grupo o una familia que viven juntos

humidity/humedad *s.* agua en el aire

hunting/cazar *v.* buscar para atrapar

I

identification (ī den tə fə kāˈ shən) *n.* form or card that proves who you are

illegal (il-lēˈ-gəl) *adj.* against the law

independence (ˌin də penˈdəns) *n.* freedom

infected (in fekˈtəd) *v.* became sick

injured (inˈjərd) *adj.* hurt

inspired (in spīˈ ərd) *v.* When people feel they want to do something.

instantly (in(t) *stənt lē) adv.* right away

instructions (in strəkˈshənz) *n.* steps that tell you how to do something

insult (inˈsəlt) *n.* hurtful action

intelligence (in teˈ lə jəns) *n.* being able to learn or solve problems

international (in tər nashˈ nəl) *adj.* many countries

interview (inˈ tər vyü) *n.* a meeting for asking questions of a person

invented (in ventˈ əd) *v.* created

I

identification/identificación *s.* forma o tarjeta que demuestra quién eres

illegal/ilegal *adj.* en contra de la ley

independence/independencia *s.* libertad

infected/infectarse *v.* enfermarse

injured/lastimado *adj.* herido

inspired/inspiraron *v.* cuando las personas sienten que quieren hacer algo

instantly/inmediatamente *adv.* sin demora

instructions/instrucciones *s.* pasos que te dicen cómo hacer algo

insult/insulto *s.* acción hiriente

intelligence/inteligencia *s.* la capacidad de aprender o de resolver problemas

international/internacional *adj.* muchos países

interview/entrevista *s.* una cita para hacerle preguntas a una persona

invented/inventó *v.* creó

island (ī-lənd) *n.* land surrounded by water

island/isla *s.* tierra que está rodeada de agua

J

J

journalist (jər' nə list) *n.* a person who writes for a newspaper

journalist/periodista *s.* una persona que escribe para un periódico

judges (jə' jəz) *n.* people who choose a winner

judges/jueces *s.* personas que escogen a un ganador

K

K

kingdoms (kiə'dəmz) *n.* lands ruled by kings or queens

kingdoms/reinos *s.* tierras gobernadas por reyes o reinas

L

L

leader (lē' dər) *n.* one who shows others what to do

leader/líder *s.* persona que enseña a los demás qué hacer

league (lēg') *n.* group of sports teams that play games against each other

league/liga *s.* grupo de equipos deportivos que juegan entre sí

liquid (li' kwəd) *n.* like water

liquid/líquido *s.* como agua

loom (lüm') *n.* machine for making cloth

loom/telar *s.* máquina para hacer tela

lucky (lə' kē) *adj.* having good things happen

lucky/afortunado *adj.* persona a la que le pasan buenas cosas

lug (ləg') *v.* to drag something that is heavy

lug/arrastrar *v.* tirar de algo que es pesado

luscious (lə' shəs) *adj.* very good to eat

luscious/exquisito *adj.* con muy buen sabor

M

M

magazine (mag'ə zēn') *n.* publication that has stories or articles

magazine/revista *s.* publicación que tiene historias o artículos

meditate ('me-də-tāt) *v.* to be still and think deeply

meditate/meditar *v.* estar inmóvil y pensar profundamente

message (me'sij) *n.* thought to be shared

message/mensaje *s.* pensamiento que se comparte

meteorite (mēˈtē əˌrīt) *n.* rock from space

miner (mīˈ nər) *n.* a worker who digs into the ground

models (mäˈ dəlz) *n.* examples

morals (morˈ əlz) *n.* beliefs about what is good and bad

mountains (maunˈ tənz) *n.* large hills or land formations

N

natural resources (naˈchə rəl rēˌsȯrs ez) *n.* things from the earth that people use

non-renewable resources (nänˈrēˈnüˈə bəl rēˌsȯrs ez) *n.* things you can use only once

notify (nōˈtə ˌfī) *v.* let know

O

obey (ō bāˈ) *v.* do what someone says

opportunities (ä pər tü ˈ nə tēz) *n.* chances for success

organized (oˈrˈgə ˌnīzd) *v.* planned all the details

P

painting (pāntˈ iŋ) *v.* creating a picture with paints

paralyzes (ˈpar ə līz is) *makes unable to move*

participate v. (pär-ti-sə-pāt,) *take part in*

passengers (paˈsən jərz) *n.* people in the car

meteorite/meteorito *s.* roca del espacio

miner/minero *s.* un trabajador que cava la tierra

models/modelos *s.* ejemplos

morals/moral *s.* creencia acerca de lo que es bueno y malo

mountains/montañas *s.* grandes colinas o formaciones de tierra

N

natural *s.* resources/recursos naturales s. cosas de la tierra que usa la gente

non-renewable *s.* resources/ recursos no renovables s. cosas que se pueden usar una sola vez

notify/notificar *v.* decir

O

obey/obedecer *v.* hacer lo que dice alguien

opportunities/oportunidades *s.* buenos momentos para algo

organized/organizó *v.* planeó todos los detalles

P

painting/pintar *v.* crear un cuadro con pinturas

paralyzes/paraliza *v.* hace que no pueda moverse

participate/participar *v.* tomar parte en

passengers/pasajeros *s.* personas en el coche

peace ('pēs) *n.* no fighting between people

peace/paz *s.* situación en la que las personas no pelean

peaceful (pēs' fəl) *adj.* calm, without fighting

peaceful/pacífico *adj.* calmado, que no pelea

peaceful (pēs' fəl) *adj.* quiet

peaceful/pacífico *adj.* tranquilo

perform (pər form') *v.* act out before an audience

perform/actuar *v.* representar enfrente de un público

picket (pi'kət) *v.* stopping others from entering a building

picket/cercar *(con piquetas)* *v.* impedir la entrada a un edificio

pilgrim (pil' grəm) *n.* someone who travels a long way

pilgrim/peregrino *s.* alguien que viaja a un lugar lejano

pitchers (pi' chərz) *n.* players who throw balls to the batter

pitchers/lanzadores *s.* jugadores que tiran la pelota al bateador

planet (pla' nət) *n.* object that moves around the sun

planet/planeta *s.* objeto que se mueve alrededor del Sol

platform (plat' form) *n.* high place for a speaker to stand on

platform/plataforma *s.* lugar alto donde se para alguien para hablar

polar bear (pō'lər ber') *n.* large white animal that lives in the snow

polar bear/oso polar *s.* animal grande y blanco que vive en la nieve

population (ˌpä pyə lā' shən) *n.* a group of people who live in a place

population/población *s.* un grupo de personas que viven en un lugar

potion (pō'shən) *n.* mixture of liquids to make medicine

potion/pócima *s.* mezcla de líquidos para hacer una medicina

precipitation (priˌsi pə tā'shən) *n.* rainfall

precipitation/precipitación *s.* lluvia

predict (pri dikt') *v.* to guess what will happen

predict/predecir *v.* suponer qué va a pasar

prejudice (pre' jə dəs) *n.* unfair opinion

prejudice/prejuicio *s.* opinión injusta

pretend (pri tend') *v.* take the role of; act like

pretend/aparentar *v.* hacer el papel; actuar

prey (prā')*n.* an animal that is hunted

prey/presa *s.* un animal que es cazado

print (print') *v.* to write in letters like the ones you see in this sentence

print/imprimir *v.* escribir letras como las que ves en esta oración

prison (priz' n) *n.* a place where people who have done something wrong must stay; jail

prison/prisión *s.* un lugar adonde deben ir las personas que han hecho algo malo; cárcel

promise (prä' məs) *v.* swear to do something

promise/prometer *v.* jurar hacer algo

protecting (prə tekt' iŋ) *v.* keeping something safe

protecting/proteger *v.* mantener algo seguro

protective (prə tek'tiv) *adj.* guard from something that could hurt or harm

protective/protector *adj.* que defiende de algo que podría lastimar o dañar

proud (praud') *adj.* pleased with

proud/orgulloso *adj.* satisfecho con algo

public (pub' lik) *adj.* for the use of all people

public/público *adj.* que lo pueden usar todos

R

R

radical (ra'di kəl) *adj.* extreme

radical/radical *adj.* extremo

rate (rāt') *v.* judge

rate/evaluar *v.* juzgar

recognized (re' kig nīzd) *v.* knew who someone was

recognized/reconoció *v.* supo quién era alguien

recycle (rē sī'kəl) *v.* to use something again

recycle/reciclar *v.* usar algo otra vez

regions (rē'jən) *n.* areas

regions/regiones *s.* áreas

remember (ri mem'bər) *v.* to think of something again

remember/recordar *v.* pensar en algo otra vez

renewable resources (rē'nü'ə bəl rē'sȯrs ez) *n.* things that you can replace

renewable resources/ recursos *renovables s.* cosas que se pueden reemplazar

require (ri kwīr) *v.* make by force or law

require/requerir *v.* hacer cumplir por la fuerza o por la ley

respect (ri spekt') *n.* a way of speaking and acting to someone who is important

respect/respeto *s.* una manera de hablar y tratar a alguien que es importante

respectful (ri spekt'fəl) *adj.* showing good manners

restrained (ri strənd') *v.* tied down

return (rē' tərn) *v.* to come back again

ripen (rī pən') *v.* to become fully grown and good to pick and eat

river ('ri-vər) *n.* large body of moving water

roast (rōst') *v.* cook over an open fire

roll (rōl') *v.* to turn over

romp (romp') *v.* play and jump

rude (rüd') *adj.* showing disrespect

rule (rül) *n.* control over people

run-down (rən' daun) *adj.* falling apart

rustling (rə' sə ling) *adj.* making a sound like moving one's hand around in a bag

respectful/respetuoso *adj.* que muestra buenos modales

restrained/inmovilizado *v.* atado

return/retornar *v.* regresar, volver

ripen/madurar *v.* crecer por completo y estar listo para comerse

river/río *s.* gran masa de agua que se mueve

roast/asar *v.* cocinar sobre fuego

roll/rodar *v.* dar vuelta

romp/retozar *v.* saltar y brincar

rude/grosero *adj.* que muestra poco respeto

rule/reinado *s.* control sobre la gente

run-down/desbaratado *adj.* que se está cayendo

rustling/crujiente *adj.* que se oye como cuando uno mete la mano en una bolsa

S

S

sailor (sā' lər) *n.* person who works on a boat

save (sāv') *v.* to free from danger

save (sāv') *v.* to protect from danger

scattered ('ska tərd) *v.* tossed or thrown in many different directions

scenery (sē' nə rē) *n.* walls and pictures on a stage that show the setting

scholar (skä' lər) *n.* well educated person

sailor/marinero *s.* persona que trabaja en un barco

save/salvar *v.* librar de un peligro

save/salvar *v.* proteger de un peligro

scattered/disperso *v.* tirado o arrojado en muchas direcciones

scenery/decorado *s.* paredes y pinturas en un escenario que muestran el ambiente

scholar/culto *s.* persona con buena educación

scratch (skrach') *v.* to rub skin

seashells (sē'shelz) *n.* hard coverings no longer needed by sea animals

secret (sē' krət) *n.* something one does not want others to know

secret (sē' krət) *n.* something one does not want others to know

segments (seg'məntz) *n.* different parts of a whole

segregation (se gri gā'shən) *n.* when different groups of people must live separately

senses (sents'ez) *n.* sight, taste, touch, hearing, smell

serious (sēr'ē əs) *adj.* thoughtful and grave

servants (sər' vəntz) *n.* people who work for and wait on other people

shivered (shiv'ərd) *v.* shook

shore (shor') *n.* where land meets the water

shrugged ('shrəgd) *v.* gave a jerk of the shoulders

shrugged (shrəg' əd) *v.* raised and lowered shoulders quickly

signature (sig'nə ,chür) *n.* how a person writes his or her own name

silk (silk') *n.* soft, thin thread

skillful (skil' fəl) *adj.* well done

sled (sled') *n.* something to sit or stand on that slides on snow

scratch/rascar *v.* frotar la piel

seashells/conchas *(marinas)* *s.* cubiertas duras que los animales marinos ya no necesitan

secret/secreto *s.* algo que uno no quiere que sepan los demás

secret/secreto *s.* algo que uno no quiere que sepan los demás

segments/segmentos *s.* diferentes partes de un todo

segregation/segregación *s.* cuando diferentes grupos de personas deben vivir separados

senses/sentidos *s.* vista, gusto, tacto, oído, olfato

serious/serio *adj.* pensativo y reservado

servants/criados *s.* personas que trabajan y sirven para otras personas

shivered/tiritó *v.* tembló

shore/orilla *s.* donde se encuentran la tierra y el agua

shrugged/encogerse *(de hombros)* *v.* contraer los hombros

shrugged/encoger *(los hombros)* *v.* subir y bajar los hombros rápidamente

signature/firma *s.* la manera como una persona escribe su nombre

silk/seda *s.* hilo suave y fino

skillful/hábil *adj.* capaz de hacer algo bien

sled/trineo *s.* algo en lo que uno se para o se sienta y que se desliza sobre la nieve

snarled (snär(-ə)ld) *v.* growled

sneaked (snēkt¹) *v.* came by secretly

sniffing (snif¹fiŋ) *v.* using one's nose to smell

snoring (snor¹ əng) *v.* the loud breathing sound when someone is asleep

society (sə sī¹ ə tē) *n.* a group of people living together

solve (solv¹) *v.* fix; find the answer

sparks (spärks¹) *n.* small burning particles in the air

spices (spīs¹ ez) *n.* pepper and other types of flavors that you add to food

spikes (spīks¹) *n.* long, pointed objects

split (¹split) *v.* broke in half; separated

sticky (sti¹ kē) *adj.* substance like glue that makes things stay together

storm (¹storm) *n.* very bad weather

strength (streŋ(k)th) *n.* power

stubborn (stə¹bərn) *adj.* does not change his ideas

subject (səb¹ jikt) *n.* what a movie or book is mostly about

successful (sək ¹səs fəl) *adj.* has done well

suffering (¹sə-fə-riŋ) *n.* experiencing difficulty

support (sə port¹) *v.* to help another

snarled/gruñó *v.* rugió

sneaked/infiltrarse *v.* llegar de manera oculta

sniffing/oler *v.* usar la nariz para sentir un olor

snoring/roncar *v.* el fuerte sonido que uno produce al respirar mientras duerme

society/sociedad *s.* un grupo de personas que viven juntas

solve/resolver *v.* arreglar, encontrar la respuesta

sparks/chispas *s.* pequeñas partículas encendidas que están en el aire

spices/especias *s.* pimienta y otros tipos de condimentos que se añaden a la comida

spikes/puntas *s.* objetos largos y afilados

split/partió *v.* rompió por la mitad, separó

sticky/pegajoso *adj.* que hace que las cosas permanezcan unidas

storm/tormenta *s.* muy mal tiempo

strength/fuerza *s.* poder

stubborn/terco *adj.* que no cambia de ideas

subject/tema *s.* el asunto principal de una película o un libro

successful/exitoso *adj.* que le ha ido bien

suffering/sufrimiento *s.* pasar por una dificultad

support/apoyar *v.* ayudar a alguien

surrounded (sə' raund əd) *v.* closed in on all sides

survey (sər'vā) *n.* a list of questions

suspected (sə spek'təd) *v.* thought that someone had done something wrong

swing (swing') *n.* seat that moves back and forth

surrounded/rodeó *v.* encerró por todos lados

survey/encuesta *s.* una lista de preguntas

suspected/sospechó *v.* pensó que alguien había hecho algo incorrecto

swing/columpio *s.* asiento que se mueve hacia adelante y hacia atrás

T

T

tale (tāl') *n.* a story

tamed (tāmd') *v.* made a wild animal follow orders

tangy (taŋ-ē') *adj.* strong-tasting

tax (taks) *n.* money collected by the government

teams (tēmz') *n.* groups of people that work together

tent (tent') *n.* shelter used when camping

thief (thēf') *n.* one who steals

thirst (thərst') *n.* needing something to drink

threatened (thre'tənd) *v.* promised to

tomb (tüm') *n.* a room for a dead body

town (town') *n.* small city

toxic (täk'sik) *adj.* poisonous

traditional (trə di' shən əl) *adj.* in the way that people have always done it

tale/cuento *s.* una historia

tamed/domó *v.* hizo que un animal salvaje obedeciera sus órdenes

tangy/penetrante *adj.* con sabor fuerte

tax/impuesto *s.* dinero que recoge el gobierno

teams/equipos *s.* grupos de personas que trabajan juntas

tent/tienda *(de campaña)* *s.* refugio que se usa al acampar

thief/ladrón *s.* alguien que roba

thirst/sed *s.* necesidad de beber algo

threatened/amenazó *v.* prometió

tomb/tumba *s.* un cuarto para el cuerpo de un muerto

town/pueblo *s.* pequeña ciudad

toxic/tóxico *adj.* venenoso

traditional/tradicional *adj.* de la manera como la gente lo ha hecho siempre

traditions (trə di' shənz) *n.* cultural beliefs, opinions and practices

trap ('trap) *v.* catch

trespasser ('tres-pəs-ər) *n.* someone who came without permission

trust (trəst') *v.* believe; think

trust (trəst') *v.* to believe in

tuition (tə wi' shən) *n.* the money a student must pay for classes

traditions/tradiciones *s.* creencias, opiniones y prácticas culturales

trap/atrapar *v.* capturar, agarrar

trespasser/intruso *s.* alguien que llegó sin permiso

trust/confiar *v.* creer; pensar

trust/confiar *v.* creer

tuition/colegiatura *s.* el dinero que un estudiante debe pagar por sus clases

U

U

unfair (ˌən fer') *adj.* not just or right

utensils (yu̇ ten' səlz) *n.* tools for eating

unfair/injusto *adj.* que no es justo o correcto

utensils/utensilios *s.* herramientas para comer

V

V

vacation (vā kā' shən) *n.* time off from work or school

variety (və rī' ə tē) *n.* different kinds

vehicles (vē'ə kəlz) *n.* cars trucks, or other types of transportation

venom (ve'n əm) *n.* poison

venomous (ve'nə məs) *adj poisonous*

veterinarians (və tə rə'ner ē əns) *animal doctors*

volcano (väl kā'nō) *n.* hole in the Earth that releases lava

vote (vōt') *v.* to make a choice

vacation/vacaciones *s.* período de descanso del trabajo o de la escuela

variety/variedad *s.* diferentes tipos

vehicles/vehículos *s.* coches, camiones u otros tipos de transporte

venom/veneno *s.* sustancia que daña la salud

venomous/venenoso *adj.* que daña la salud

veterinarians/veterinarios *s.* médicos para animales

volcano/volcán *s.* hoyo en la Tierra del que sale lava

vote/votar *v.* hacer una elección

W

wagon (wa' gən) *n.* a cart that is pulled by animals

waves (wāvz') *n.* moving water

webs (webz') *n.* thin structures made by spiders

wheezes (wēz') *v.* breathes in a noisy way

wide (wīd') *adj.* far apart from side to side

wisdom ('wiz-dəm) *n.* deep understanding of many things

wise (wīz') *adj.* smart

woods (woodz') *n.* many trees in an area

W

wagon/carreta *s.* un carro que es tirado por animales

waves/olas *s.* agua que se mueve

webs/telarañas *s.* estructuras finas que hacen las arañas

wheezes/resuella *v.* respira ruidosamente

wide/ancho *adj.* con mucho espacio de un lado a otro

wisdom/sabiduría *s.* profundo conocimiento de muchas cosas

wise/sabio *adj.* inteligente

woods/bosque *s.* muchos árboles en un área

INDEX OF AUTHORS AND TITLES

ACKNOWLEDGMENTS

Text Credits

Adaptation of "The Sand Castle" by Alma Luz Villanueva, reprinted by permission of the author.

"Will there really be a 'Morning'" Reprinted by permission of the publishers and the Trustees of Amherst College from *The Poems of Emily Dickinson,* Thomas H. Johnson, ed., Cambridge, Mass: The Belknap Press of Harvard University Press, Copyright © 1951, 1955, 1979, 1983 by the President and Fellows of Harvard College.

"Campfire" reprinted with the permission of Margaret K. McElderry Books, an imprint of Simon & Schuster Children's Publishing Division, from *A Suitcase of Seaweed and Other Poems* by Janet S. Wong. Copyright © 1996 Janet S. Wong.

"Loo-Wit: The Firekeeper" by Joseph Bruchac. Adapted and reprinted by permission of Barbara S. Kouts.

Image Credits

1 Tanya Constantine/Getty Images; 3 (l to r, t to b)Simon Jarratt/CORBIS, Luca Tettoni/CORBIS, Jeff Spielman/Getty Images, J. James/zefa/CORBIS, Christine Mariner/Design Pics/CORBIS, Archivo Iconografico S.A./CORBIS; 4 Pete Turner/Getty Images; 5 ABN Stock Images/Alamy Images; 6 Maurizio Gambarini/CORBIS; 7 Getty Images; 8 Getty Images; 9 (l to r, t to b)Ruaridh Stewart/ZUMA/CORBIS, Michael Christopher Brown/CORBIS, bilder-lounge/CORBIS, Steven Clevenger/CORBIS, moodboard/CORBIS, Comstock/CORBIS, Mika/zefa/CORBIS, Michael A. Keller/CORBIS; 10 Getty Images; 11 Getty Images; 12 Time & Life Pictures/Getty Images; 13 Robert van der Hilst/CORBIS; 15 (l to r, t to b)Josef Fankhauser/Getty Images, John-Francis Bourke/zefa/CORBIS, Solus-Veer/CORBIS, Ron Chapple/CORBIS, Grove Pashley/Getty Images, Mango Productions/CORBIS, Heide Benser/zefa/CORBIS, Normal/plainpicture/CORBIS; 16-17 American School/Getty Images; 18 (t to b)Archive Holdings Inc./Getty Images, Dave Bartruff/CORBIS, Jules Frazier/Getty Images; 19 Museum of History and Industry/CORBIS; 21 Douglas Grundy/Getty Images; 22 Christopher Stevenson/Getty Images; 23 Layne Kennedy/CORBIS; 24 Bettmann/CORBIS; 25 Bread and Butter/Getty Images; 27 (l to r, t to b)Adrian Sherratt/Alamy Images, Blend Images/Jupiter Images, Michael Dwyer/Alamy Images, Photo Network/Alamy Images, A. T. Willett/Alamy Images, Luca DiCecco/Alamy Images, Keith Leighton/Alamy Images, AFP/Getty Images; 28-34 Lee Chapman; 35 (l)Getty Images, (r)AFP/Getty Images; 37 (l to r, t to b)Dale C. Spartas/CORBIS, Steve Schapiro/CORBIS, Image Source Black/Getty Images, ICHIRO/Getty Images, Baerbel Schmidt/Getty Images, Kate Mitchell/zefa/CORBIS, Digital Vision/SuperStock, Compassionate Eye

Foundation/Jonathan Ross/Getty Images; **38** Reuters/CORBIS; **39** Getty Images; **40** Reuters/CORBIS; **41** Getty Images; **43** (l to r, t to b)Blend Images/Jupiter Images, Studio Eye/CORBIS, Chuck Franklin/Alamy Images, Photographer's Choice/Punchstock, Mark Karrass/CORBIS, Brand X Pictures/SuperStock, US ARMY HANDOUT/epa/CORBIS, Mervyn Rees/Alamy Images; **44** Owen Franken/CORBIS; **45** Ausloeser/zefa/CORBIS; **46** Blend Images/Alamy Images; **53** SW Productions/Getty Images; **55** (l to r, t to b)Sheer Photo, Inc/Getty Images, Norman Jung/zefa/CORBIS, Thom Lang/CORBIS, Didier Robcis/CORBIS, ICHIRO/Getty Images, Neil Overy/Getty Images, Varie/Alt/CORBIS, Tom Grill/Getty Images; **56** Ken Kaminesky/Take 2 Productions/CORBIS; **57** (l)Brand X/CORBIS, (r)Leonard de Selva/CORBIS; **59** (l)Jutta Klee/CORBIS, (r)M. Timothy O'Keefe/Alamy Images; **60** Andrew McCaul/Getty Images; **61** Frank Lukasseck/CORBIS; **63** (l to r, t to b)AFP/Getty Images, Winfried Wisniewski/zefa/CORBIS, PoodlesRock/CORBIS, Pearl Bucknall/LOOP IMAGES/Loop Images/CORBIS, Richard Naude/Alamy Images, Bob Stefko/Getty Images, Remi Benali/CORBIS, Michael Nicholson/CORBIS; **64** Getty Images; **65** Keren Su/CORBIS; **66** Danny Lehman/CORBIS; **67** Imagemore Co., Ltd./CORBIS; **68 69** Keren Su/CORBIS; **70** Keren Su/CORBIS; **71** (t)Yang Liu/CORBIS, (b)Jim Craigmyle/CORBIS; **73** (l to r, t to b)James Nazz/CORBIS, Ansgar Photography/zefa/CORBIS, Jutta Klee/CORBIS, Mike Theiss/Ultimate Chase/CORBIS, Tim Tadder/CORBIS, Allison Michael Orenstein/Getty Images, Tanya Constantine/Getty Images, Mark A. Johnson/CORBIS; **74** (t)Darren Greenwood/Design Pics/CORBIS, (b)Brown W. Cannon III/Getty Images; **75** (t to b)Tim Pannell/CORBIS, Niall Benvie/CORBIS, Catherine Ledner/Getty Images; **76** (t)Oswald Eckstein/zefa/CORBIS, (b)David Woods/CORBIS; **77** The Irish Image Collection/CORBIS; **78** (t)moodboard/CORBIS, (b)Jon Arnold/JAI/CORBIS; **80** (l to r, t to b)Don Farrall/Getty Images, Reuters/CORBIS, Natural Selection David Ponton/Design Pics/CORBIS, Stephen Frink/Getty Images, The Studio Dog/Getty Images, Getty Images, Photographers Choice/SuperStock, Peter Dazeley/Getty Images; **81** Stuart Gregory/Getty Images; **82** Martin Barraud/Getty Images; **84** Joe Cornish/Arcaid/CORBIS; **85** Denis Scott/CORBIS; **86** Kirk Treakle/Alamy Images; **87** (l to r, t to b) David Madison/CORBIS, Diego Uchitel/Getty Images, Blaine Harrington III/CORBIS, Tony Latham/zefa/CORBIS, Owaki-Kulla/CORBIS, Bertrand Gardel/Hemis/CORBIS, Denis Scott/CORBIS, The Gallery Collection/CORBIS; **90** Ashley Cooper/CORBIS; **91** Denis Scott/CORBIS; **92** Frank Lukasseck/CORBIS; **93** Lloyd Kenneth Jr. Townsend/National Geographic Image Collection, Punchstock; **94** (l ro r)Henny Ray Abrams/Reuters/CORBIS, Peter Holst/Getty Images, Jennifer Brown/Star Ledger/CORBIS; **95** Gallo Images/CORBIS; **97** (l to r, t to b)Rolf Bruderer/CORBIS, LWA/Getty Images, Bruno Levy/zefa/CORBIS, Christine Mariner/Design Pics/CORBIS, Peter M. Fisher/CORBIS, Lauren Nicole/Getty Images, Roy Mehta/Getty Images, Peter Adams/CORBIS; **98-104** Felipe Ugalde; **105** Manda Nicholls/Alamy

Bloomimage/Getty Images; **179** (l to r, t to b) Michael Blann/Getty Images, David Harrigan/Getty Images, Jim Craigmyle/Corbis, Don Mason/CORBIS, ColorBlind Images/Getty Images, Richard Hutchings/Corbis; **180** Chris Collins/zefa/Corbis; **181** Dorling Kindersley/Getty Images; **182** (t to b)Inti St. Clair/Getty Images, fStop/Alamy Images; **183** Erik Dreyer/Getty Images; **184** (l to r, t to b) Reuters/CORBIS, Martin Ruetschi/Keystone/Corbis, Siri Stafford/Getty Images, Anna Peisl/zefa/Corbis, Cristian Baitg/Getty Images, Ariel Skelley/Getty Images, Mike Kemp/Getty Images, David Michael Zimmerman/Corbis; **185** DLILLC/Corbis **186** (t to b)Rin Tsukioka/ailead/Getty Images, Punchstock; **187** Katarina Carlgren/Alamy Images; **188** Getty Images; **189** John Fiordalisi/Getty Images; **191** (l to r, t to b)Floresco Productions/Corbis, Heidi & Hans-Jurgen Koch/Getty Images, Aaron Horowitz/CORBIS, W. Perry Conway/CORBIS, Don Hammond/Design Pics/Corbis, Cultura/Corbis, M. Taghi/zefa/Corbis, Joe McDonald/CORBIS; **192** David A. Northcott/CORBIS; **194** Pablo Corral V/CORBIS; **196** (l to r, t to b)Sonja Pacho/zefa/Corbis, Wim Klomp/Foto Natura/Getty Images, George B. Diebold/Corbis, Matthias Kulka/zefa/Corbis, Poisson d'Avril/photocuisine/Corbis, Frans Lanting/Corbis, Ivan Vdovin/JAI/CORBIS, Martin Ruegner/Getty Images; **197** Todd Gipstein Christian Schmidt/zefa/Corbis; **199** Peter Cade/Getty Images; **201** (l to r, t to b)Con Tanasiuk/Design Pics/CORBIS, Alessandra Schellnegger/zefa/CORBIS, Raimund Koch/Getty Images, Kate Mitchell/zefa/CORBIS, Paul Hardy/CORBIS, Simon Jarratt/CORBIS; **202-** **204** Nancy Speir; **205** (l to r, t to b)Nice One Productions/CORBIS, FK PHOTO/CORBIS, Nice One Productions/CORBIS, Image Source/CORBIS, Craig Lovell/CORBIS, Bob Sacha/CORBIS, Charles Bowman/Robert Harding World Imagery/CORBIS, Mike Powell/Getty Images; **206** (t to b)Marco Simoni/Getty Images, Italian School/Getty Images; **207** (t to b)Adrian Buck/Alamy Images, Adrian Buck/Alamy Images; **209** Adrian Buck/Alamy Images; **210** IML Image Group Ltd/Alamy Images; **211** Radius Images/Alamy Images; **213** (l to r, t to b)Greg Hinsdale/CORBIS, CJ Gunther/epa/CORBIS, Tango/zefa/CORBIS, moodboard/CORBIS, Schlegelmilch/CORBIS, Steven Vidler/Eurasia Press/CORBIS, Joaquin Palting/CORBIS, David Aubrey/CORBIS; **214** (t to b)Getty Images, Guy Motil/CORBIS, C Squared Studios/Getty Images; **215** Getty Images; **216 217** Time & Life Pictures/Getty Images; **218** (l to r, t to b)Jim Vecchi/CORBIS, Robert Michael/CORBIS, Jim Vecchi/CORBIS, Ariel Skelley/CORBIS, Randy Faris/CORBIS, Natalie Fobes/CORBIS; **219** Photographer's Choice/Getty Images; **219-220** Derrick Chow; **227** Alamy Images; **229** (l to r, t to b)Jose Luis Pelaez Inc/Getty Images, Antonio M. Rosario/Getty Images, AGStockUSA, Inc./Alamy Images, Jeffrey L. Rotman/CORBIS, Chad Ehlers/Getty Images, Leo Mason/CORBIS, Stuart Westmorland/Getty Images, P. Broze & A. Chederros/Getty Images; **230** (t to b)Peter Beck/CORBIS, TNT MAGAZINE/Alamy Images; **231** Martin Harvey/CORBIS; **232** (t to b)Tom Stewart/CORBIS, Chris Rose/Alamy Images, Pick and Mix Images/Alamy Images; **233** Jose Luis Pelaez, Inc./

Images; **295** (l to r)Mimmo Jodice/ CORBIS, Bettmann/CORBIS; **296 297** Michael Maslan Historic Photographs/ CORBIS; **296** Adrees Latif/Reuters/ CORBIS; **297** The Bridgeman Art Library, Bettmann/CORBIS; **298** (t to b)Karen Huntt/CORBIS, Gianni Dagli Orti/CORBIS, Bettmann/CORBIS; **299** Turbo/zefa/CORBIS; **301** (l to r, t to b) Kelly Redinger/Design Pics/CORBIS, UpperCut Images/SuperStock, visage media services pvt ltd/Alamy Images, Serge Kozak/zefa/CORBIS, Punchstock, moodboard/CORBIS, david gregs/ Alamy Images, Dennis MacDonald/ Alamy Images; **302** D. Hurst/Alamy Images, **303** (l)Photodisc/SuperStock, (r)D. Hurst/Alamy Images; **304** Tony Watson/Alamy Images; **305** Comstock/ SuperStock; **306** Digital Vision/Alamy Images; **307** PhotoAlto/SuperStock; **308** Jean Cazals/Getty Images; **309** Ned Frisk Photography/CORBIS; **310** (t)Camille Tokerud/Getty Images, (b)Jim West/Alamy Images; **311** (t)Photodisc/ Alamy Images, (b)Fine Art Photographic Library/CORBIS; **312** (t)Photodisc/Alamy Images, (b)Nicolas Randall/Alamy Images; **313** (l to r)Burazin/Getty Images, Peter Arnold, Inc./Alamy Images, Joe Tree/Alamy Images; **314** Joseph Sohm/Visions of America/CORBIS; **315** Kim Karpeles/ Alamy Images; **316** D. Hurst/Alamy Images; **317** (l to r, t to b)Bettmann/ CORBIS, Horacio Villalobos/CORBIS, Reuters/CORBIS, Jean-Michel Turpin/ Sygma/CORBIS; **319** (l to r, t to b)Bettmann/CORBIS, Don Hammond/ Design Pics/CORBIS, Thom Lang/ CORBIS, Robert Michael/CORBIS, JLP/ Jose L. Pelaez/CORBIS, Micha Pawlitzki/zefa/CORBIS, David Madison/ CORBIS, Bahar Yurukoglu/zefa/CORBIS;

320 Getty Images; **321** Alan Schein Photography/CORBIS; **322 323** (l to r)Per-Anders Pettersson/Getty Images, Dorling Kindersley Getty Images, Reuters/CORBIS; **324** (t to b)Bob Krist/ CORBIS, Andrew Gombert/epa/CORBIS, Getty Images; **325** AFP/Getty Images; **326** Per-Anders Pettersson/Getty Images; **327** Strauss/Curtis/CORBIS; **329** (l to r, t to b)C.F. Everest/Brand X/ CORBIS, Matthias Kulka/zefa/CORBIS, James Emmerson/Robert Harding World Imagery/CORBIS, Punchstock, Owen Franken/CORBIS, Leland Bobbe/ Getty Images, Normal/plainpicture/ CORBIS, Chemistry/Getty Images; **330-334** Stephen Aiken; **335** Philip and Karen Smith/Getty Images; **337** (l to r, t to b)PhotoAlto/Alamy Images, Craig Lovell/CORBIS, Arnold Bell/Alamy Images, Theo Allofs/CORBIS, Clive Nichols/Arcaid/CORBIS, The McGraw-Hill Companies, Ben Fink/Brand X/ CORBIS, Rick Wilking/Reuters/CORBIS; **338 339** (l to r)Lester Lefkowitz/CORBIS, Marilyn Angel Wynn/Nativestock Pictures/CORBIS; **340** (t to b)INTERFOTO Pressebildagentur/Alamy Images, Galen Rowell/Mountain Light/ Alamy Images; **341** Anders Ryman/ Alamy Images; **342** (l to r)Craig Tuttle/ CORBIS, Gary Braasch/CORBIS, Chase Jarvis/CORBIS; **343** (l to r, t to b)Christina Kennedy/Alamy Images, David Murray/Getty Images, Mira/ Alamy Images, Rusty Hill/Getty Images, Jeffrey Hamilton/Getty Images, Richard Drury/Getty Images, FogStock/Alamy Images, Bloomimage/Getty Images; **344-346** Derrick Chow.